Welcome to the
BlackBerry PlayBook

The launch of a BlackBerry tablet computer to rival the likes of Apple's iPad and the Samsung Galaxy Tab has created a great deal of excitement among existing BlackBerry smartphone users and technology consumers alike.

And there's no doubt that RIM's BlackBerry PlayBook brings something new to the table. As yet it may not be able to send and receive emails on the fly or synchronise data when not connected to your BlackBerry, but it's probably the most secure tablet available.

For existing BlackBerry smartphone users it's the perfect tablet option. However, the PlayBook's appeal goes way beyond business users. It's the perfect size to fit in a bag, yet the screen is big enough to display stunning video content. Thousands of apps are on offer; many of them are business focused, as you'd expect, but huge numbers of entertainment apps are also available, ranging from games such as Tetris and Need For Speed to colouring books for kids. And the web browser is the best we've seen on a tablet device, allowing you to watch YouTube videos in all their full Flash-filled glory.

Ultimate Guide to BlackBerry PlayBook has been designed to help you get the most out of your new tablet. It will guide you through setting up your PlayBook, as well as showcasing some of its hidden features. Visual tours and step-by-step tutorials will get beginners up and running quickly, and we've also included sections on security and app development for more advanced users. It's the perfect companion for anyone who's bought – or is thinking of buying – a BlackBerry PlayBook.

We've loved using the BlackBerry PlayBook, and we hope we can share that passion with you.

Enjoy!

Clare Hopping,
Editor

BLACKBERRY PLAYBOOK

EDITOR
Clare Hopping

CONTRIBUTORS
Simon Bisson, Mary Branscombe,
Maggie Holland

ART & DESIGN
Art Editor Dean Reynolds

ADVERTISING
Advertising Manager Martin Lynch

MANAGEMENT

MagBooks Manager Dharmesh Mistry
020 7907 6100
dharmesh_mistry@dennis.co.uk
Operations Director Robin Ryan
Group Advertising Director Julian Lloyd-Evans
Newstrade Director David Barker
Chief Operating Officer Brett Reynolds
Group Finance Director Ian Leggett
Chief Executive James Tye
Chairman Felix Dennis

MAGBOOK

The MagBook brand is a trademark of
Dennis Publishing Ltd. 30 Cleveland St,
London W1T 4JD. Company registered in
England. All material © Dennis Publishing
Ltd, licensed by Felden 2011, and may not
be reproduced in whole or part without the
consent of the publishers.

Ultimate Guide to BlackBerry PlayBook
ISBN 1-907779-93-0

Licensing To license this product, please
contact Hannah Heagney on +44 (0) 20 7907
6134 or email hannah_heagney@dennis.co.uk

Liability While every care was taken during the
production of this MagBook, the publishers
cannot be held responsible for the accuracy
of the information or any consequence
arising from it. Dennis Publishing takes no
responsibility for the companies advertising
in this MagBook. The paper used within this
MagBook is produced from sustainable fibre,
manufactured by mills with a valid chain of
custody. Printed at BGP, Bicester, Oxon.

Contents

The eagerly anticipated BlackBerry PlayBook has finally arrived, but what does it offer that its rivals don't? We go behind the shiny façade to find out

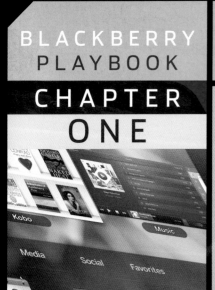

BLACKBERRY PLAYBOOK

CHAPTER ONE

INTRODUCTION

What is the
BlackBerry PlayBook?

n January 2010, Apple launched a new tablet computer that would revolutionise the way people use mobile devices.

The iPad wasn't a smartphone like the iPhone, but a hybrid device that placed it somewhere between a netbook and a smartphone. It had the same connectivity solutions as the iPhone, but with a much larger screen for performing tasks you'd normally be able to carry out only on a PC.

Research In Motion (RIM), the company behind the popular BlackBerry smartphone, responded to this innovative device with the BlackBerry PlayBook. Although aimed at a slightly different market to the iPad, the PlayBook will enter a concentrated market, currently dominated by the iPad and tablets running the Android operating system.

The BlackBerry PlayBook was first demonstrated in October 2010 by RIM and has since been part of the tablet buzz. So what does it actually offer?

"RIM set out to engineer the best professional-grade tablet in the industry, with cutting-edge hardware features and one of the world's most robust and flexible operating systems," said Mike Lazaridis, president and co-CEO at RIM.

"The BlackBerry PlayBook solidly hits the mark, with industry-leading power, true multitasking, uncompromised web browsing and high-performance multimedia," he continued.

"We're not trying to dumb down the internet for a mobile device. What we've done is bring up mobile devices to the level of desktop computers."

First and foremost, the PlayBook offers secure access to a BlackBerry user's email, calendars and BlackBerry Messenger while on the move.

Although aimed at business users, it includes some pretty impressive hardware, including a 7-inch 1,024x600-pixel screen and a 1GHz Cortex-A9 dual-core processor.

On the back of the PlayBook, you'll find a 5-megapixel camera, while the front offers a 3-megapixel camera for high-quality video calling. US versions of the PlayBook will ship with 4G support, but in the UK we're limited to Wi-Fi or 3G connectivity.

Like the iPad 2, HDMI capabilities mean the BlackBerry PlayBook can be hooked up to an HD TV, although it doesn't require a proprietary cable to work as the HDMI-out option on the iPad does.

The BlackBerry PlayBook measures 130x194x10mm and weighs 425g, making it one of the lightest tablets available. It runs on BlackBerry's Tablet OS, which is based upon the QNX Neutrino kernel. This tablet-specific platform allows for apps to run on Adobe AIR and HTML 5.

Unlike many tablets, including the iPad, it can also display Flash content using the 10.1 Player – which will be very handy for browsing web pages.

The PlayBook's user interface is completely different to that of BlackBerry handsets, even those running on the latest edition of BlackBerry's OS. Multitasking happens from the homescreen, with each open app displaying as a miniature page. Everything is much more fluid and consumer-friendly compared to the complicated BlackBerry smartphone OS.

With an appeal that stretches beyond RIM's traditional business market and one of the highest specifications of any tablet available, the BlackBerry PlayBook looks to have a bright future.

Introduction

Inside
BlackBerry Tablet OS

RIM, the company responsible for the iconic BlackBerry smartphone, has created a completely new operating system for the BlackBerry PlayBook.

BlackBerry Tablet OS is based on QNX Neutrino RTOS, a hugely flexible operating system that's perfect for multitasking and application development. RIM has applied its own interface to QNX Neutrino to ensure it's easy to use and responsive on a tablet.

QNX has been widely used in a number of applications, ranging from in-car entertainment and hands-free solutions to medical testing and space centre use.

WHAT IS QNX?

QNX is a microkernel-based OS. This means that, unlike other mobile-based operating systems, it works by running most operations via small tasks, which are known as servers.

Other operating systems run using the monolithic kernel model, where the actual operating system is a large operation, or task, with other operations running on it as smaller tasks.

The way QNX works allows developers to switch off individual functions or servers if they don't want that feature in a particular application or form without physically changing the platform.

The only functions the QNX kernel includes are CPU scheduling, interprocess communication, interrupt redirection and timers.

QNX Neutrino, the version used by BlackBerry's tablet, supports symmetric multiprocessing and bound multiprocessing (BMP), which allows developers to lock selected threads to selected CPUs.

HOW IS IT USED?

QNX is one of the most flexible systems available, which is one of the reasons RIM decided to use it as the basis of its tablet operating system. It's already used for a number of applications you would probably never imagine, including processes for the space station, government defence systems, medical devices and in-car systems developed for both high-end and low-end models.

Here we take a closer look at some examples of where QNX has been used.

NEPTEC LASER CAMERA SYSTEM (LCS)

This 3D laser scanner can detect tiny fractures in the space shuttle's heat shield, so is vital in protecting the shuttle crew's safety.

The technology can detect holes in the shuttle even if they're only a few millimeters in size, and can also help NASA researchers examine how heat can affect the space shuttle. It was first used on the Discovery space shuttle on its 2005 mission.

BMW CONNECTEDDRIVE WITH SMARTPHONE EMAIL AND MESSAGING CONNECTIVITY

BMW ConnectedDrive is an in-car system that enables drivers listen to emails from Bluetooth-connected phones while they're driving. It can also display calendar entries, text messages, call and contact lists and memos from a Bluetooth-connected device.

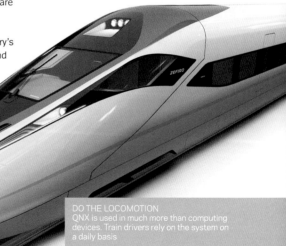

DO THE LOCOMOTION
QNX is used in much more than computing devices. Train drivers rely on the system on a daily basis

ENERGY

QNX technology controls thousands of power-generation systems worldwide, from wind turbines and hydroelectric plants to nuclear stations.

QNX-based power-grid simulators help utility companies generate electricity from solar panels, wind farms and other renewable energy sources.

SHOPPING

QNX is used for both online and high street shopping to deliver goods to customers. Amazon relies on QNX-based warehouse automation systems to move products around its warehouses and supply them to its customers.

Many other high-street retailers use QNX-based warehouse systems to move products from factories into shops.

TV AND FILMS

It's not all about big business and dull work applications with QNX. The technology is also used to control television stations, deliver cable signals on services such as Virgin and BT and to power universal remote controls so you can change the TV channel, pause a Bluray movie or turn the volume up when you're playing a console game.

And bear in mind the next time you watch a film that QNX technology has most probably been used to create the special effects. It powers motion-control systems that create the spectacular special effects and stunts see in Hollywood movies.

TRANSPORT

In addition to controlling in-car entertainment systems and damage warning systems, QNX is also widely used in the aviation industry, particularly in pilot-training simulators and air-traffic control systems around the world.

QNX-based navigation and radar systems help boats navigate through fog, bad weather and narrow estuaries, whether it's an enormous cruise ship or a small fishing boat. It's also used in the railway industry, where it controls locomotives and helps coordinate rail traffic.

WORK AND PLAY
QNX systems are used in a wide range of environments, including the energy industry, Amazon's warehouse systems, cable TV services and car manufacturing

MEDICAL USE

The QNX platform is used by hospitals around the world to power diagnostic devices such as ECG machines, angiography systems, cardiac monitors and bone-density analysers.

Scanners can detect defects in a variety of medical products. QNX-based cancer treatment devices use proton beams to target tumours without damaging nearby organs, and it's used in laser eye surgery too.

WHY IS QNX SO POPULAR?

The main advantage of using QNX is that it performs multitasking operations more efficiently than other platforms. There's almost no limit to how many applications can run in tandem, as they're all treated as individual operations and don't rely on a central core to work and save space.

One of the benefits of QNX for a mobile platform is that it can offer full web capabilities in a browser. Because each operation works independently, it's fast – so you can integrate memory-consuming features such as tabs on the same page and full Flash for playing video within a browser.

QNX supports multiple users just as a desktop OS does, meaning child-protection features and sensitive data protection can be implemented by having a password-protected separate account set up for each user.

One of the things RIM hasn't previously been able to implement effectively within its mobile OS is applications. Although BlackBerry App World has seen some success, the QNX platform offers flexible app development, allowing developers to produce software using the Adobe Air, Java and WebKit environments.

WILL QNX BE ROLLED OUT ACROSS OTHER BLACKBERRY SMARTPHONES?

For a smartphone to run on a QNX-based system, the device must include a dual-core processor. There are rumours that the QNX-based operating system will be rolled out across BlackBerry smartphones in the form of BlackBerry OS 7 later in the year, but at the time of going to press this hadn't been confirmed.

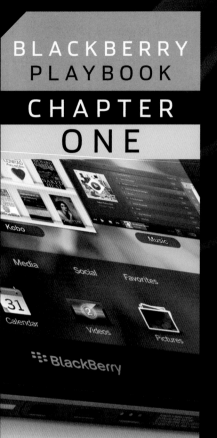

Introduction

BlackBerry Tablet OS
Alternatives

ANDROID 3.0 HONEYCOMB

Android is probably the most open tablet operating system available. This shows in every aspect of its interface, from the customisation options to multitasking and application development.

USER INTERFACE

There are two kinds of interface in Android. The first is what is known as Vanilla Android. This is the more plain UI that applies to most Android tablets.

As standard, you'll find five homescreens that can be customised with an almost limitless number of active widgets, folders and applications.

For example, from the homescreen, you can view your Twitter and Facebook feeds. If you prefer, you can group your social-networking applications into a folder and launch the applications via the folder.

Different Android 'skins' (such as those found on HTC Sense or Motorola's Motoblur) have varying numbers of homescreens and different functionality. They also have different preinstalled applications. HTC Sense, for example, features Friend Stream, a unified social-networking feed.

Just as there is on the BlackBerry Tablet OS, all Android devices include a drop-down connectivity screen that displays open connections and allows you to turn features such as Wi-Fi, data connections and Bluetooth on and off.

MULTITASKING

Android devices all integrate multitasking, although it's easier to use on some models than others.

The Vanilla Android Honeycomb firmware has overhauled its multitasking capabilities, making it much easier to operate and view all your open and recent apps.

An onscreen button brings up a view of recent apps. This shows exactly what the app looks like, whether a page is open in the browser, a real-time friend feed or the current level in a game.

APPS AND DEVELOPMENT

Android has one of the most open environments for creating, submitting and buying apps, although this hasn't always worked to Google's advantage. There have been a number of malware attacks on Android devices in recent months that demonstrate a need for some kind of regulation process.

At the time of writing, almost anyone can develop an application for Android and submit it to the App Market. The Market isn't moderated by Google, but by Android users.

Apps aren't signed as they are on BlackBerry or Symbian, so although it's attractive to smaller developers, it leaves a massive security hole.

There are currently more than 100,000 apps in Android's App Market.

APPLE iOS

Apple iOS is the platform used on the iPhone and iPad. Although the basis of the operating system is the same for both devices, a number of tweaks have been made to the OS to optimise it for the iPad's larger screen.

USER INTERFACE

The iOS user interface isn't as feature-rich as many of the other tablet operating systems on the market, but it is one of the most popular because of its simplicity and attractive design, just like the iPad itself.

Apps are displayed as icons on the homescreens, but they're not active so you can't view your friend feed or preview emails as you can on other platforms.

XOOM INTO FOCUS
The Motorola Xoom runs on Android Honeycomb (OS 3.0), one of the most open operating systems around

Compared to other platforms where you choose the apps you want shown on your homescreens, all of them will be displayed unless you decide to organise them differently. Arguably, however, it's quicker for this, with the transition between homescreens and apps extremely fast.

Apple introduced the ability to add folders with iOS 4. To create a folder, you need only to drag and drop the icons on top of each other. However, you can't add files to folders, which you can do on most other platforms.

MULTITASKING

Multitasking was one of the features added to the Apple iPad operating system with iOS 4.2. However, Apple's multitasking is still not full multitasking as seen on BlackBerry, Android and WebOS devices. Instead of apps running in the background at the same time, they pause when you move between them.

A number of apps can run in tandem, though; for example, you can listen to music while writing a document with Pages.

APPS AND DEVELOPMENT

The Apple App Store is by far the most advanced store for applications. With more than 350,000 apps available for the iPhone and 65,000 for the iPad, more money is made on this platform than any other. The success of the iPad has only increased the popularity of the store, with huge numbers of apps downloaded on a daily basis.

The App Store also has the strictest policy for developers. Applications have to be approved by Apple before they are made available for download, and many apps are rejected.

WEBOS

WebOS was developed by Palm, but after that company's demise last year, HP has taken over development and its first devices are now available.

The HP TouchPad was the first tablet to launch on the operating system, and although it takes a lot of influence from the mobile OS, it takes things to a further level, making it work perfectly on a larger screen.

USER INTERFACE

The WebOS platform first appeared on the Palm Pre, a handheld device announced three years ago and released around a year later.

WebOS is based upon cards. These are mini-versions of each page or app and are navigated through using swipes and flicks. To close applications or pages, you simply flick the cards on the screen.

WebOS is an easy UI to use and faster than the Android operating system. You can switch between apps quickly, and a launcher screen makes opening your programs a tap away.

However, the UI isn't as customisable as Android, and is probably more similar to the BlackBerry and Apple platforms in this sense.

MULTITASKING

Multitasking is effortless on the WebOS platform. The cards display on the task screen, where you can flick between them and re-order them according to their importance.

Switching is fast and closing apps even faster, with apps running together in true multitasking style.

APPS AND DEVELOPMENT

WebOS is probably the least developed in terms of applications. In September 2010, just 4,000 apps were available for the operating system.

As yet, HP has not announced whether these applications will work on WebOS 3.0, the version used on the HP TouchPad.

The beta SDK for HP WebOS 2.0 launched following the announcement of the HP Veer and Pre 3, but at the time of writing there was no word on when the WebOS 3.0 SDK would be released.

::: BlackBerry

History of the
BlackBerry

RIM 957 Wireless

BlackBerry 7290

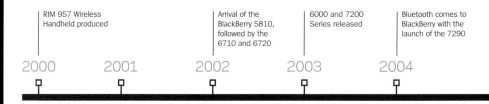

2000	2001	2002	2003	2004
RIM 957 Wireless Handheld produced		Arrival of the BlackBerry 5810, followed by the 6710 and 6720	6000 and 7200 Series released	Bluetooth comes to BlackBerry with the launch of the 7290

Research In Motion – more commonly known as RIM – was set up more than 25 years ago by engineering students Mike Lazaridis (now co-chief executive of the company) and Douglas Fregin in Canada in the mid-1980s.

The first products produced by the company were solutions and devices for the Mobitex wireless, packet-switched, data communications network in North America.

In 1996, RIM's first personal communications device was launched. The Inter@ctive Pager was a two-way messaging device for general use and quickly became popular among business professionals in several sectors, including healthcare and financial services.

The RIM 950 Wireless Handheld was launched in 1996, and although it was similar to BlackBerrys we know and love today, it still relied on Mobitex. As such, its use was limited to North America.

By 2000, RIM had come up with the RIM 957 Wireless Handheld. Its large, mono display and full QWERTY keypad set the format for more than a dozen future BlackBerry devices – although the name had yet to evolve.

The BlackBerry was so named after it was suggested the keyboard buttons looked like the seeds on a strawberry. However, a team of branding language experts claimed that strawberry suggested slowness, so the name morphed into BlackBerry.

BlackBerry Bold 9700

BlackBerry PlayBook

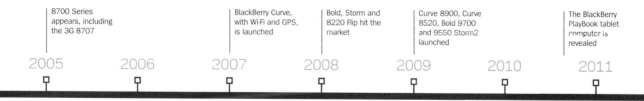

2005	2006	2007	2008	2009	2010	2011
8700 Series appears, including the 3G 8707		BlackBerry Curve, with Wi-Fi and GPS, is launched	Bold, Storm and 8220 Flip hit the market	Curve 8900, Curve 8520, Bold 9700 and 9550 Storm2 launched		The BlackBerry PlayBook tablet computer is revealed

Jump forward to the early years of the 21st century and the BlackBerry started to target consumers as well as business users. RIM launched the BlackBerry Internet Service, which allowed mobile operators to provide a service that let users pull email from POP3 and IMAP mailboxes into a push email account.

The company's device strategy also shifted. From serious business devices that lacked cutting-edge design, RIM launched the BlackBerry 6210, 6220 and 6230. These devices were half-height, mono-screen devices that were low-cost and easy to use.

By 2005, consumer demand for BlackBerry devices was almost on a par with that from business users, and more consumer-friendly handsets started to appear, including the 8700 and the short-lived 8707. This was technically RIM's first 3G device, but it wasn't widely adopted by mobile users.

The BlackBerry Curve – aimed at business users – and the Pearl – for consumers – were launched in 2007, with both handsets receiving updates that included GPS and Wi-Fi. A year later, 3G returned and HSDPA data was added as RIM brought the high-end Bold, touchscreen Storm and 8220 Flip handsets to the market.

2009 saw the release of the Curve 8900 (formerly codenamed the Javelin), BlackBerry Pearl 8120, BlackBerry Curve 8520 and the successors to the first-generation Bold and Storm devices in the form of the 9700 and 9550.

Enter 2010 and RIM became even more consumer-oriented. After redesigning its operating system to make it more user-friendly and tweaking it to resemble other consumer smartphone operating systems more, the company launched the BlackBerry Torch 9800. This smartphone combined a large capacitive touchscreen with a slide-out Qwerty keyboard, running on BlackBerry OS 6.

In the latter half of 2010, RIM followed cues from Apple with its iPad tablet and announced the PlayBook, a business-centric tablet, along with its QNX-based BlackBerry Tablet OS.

With its high-specification hardware and unique design, the PlayBook is a stunning piece of kit. Our guided tour puts all its features at your fingertips

THE PLAYBOOK

The PlayBook in detail

Since Apple launched the iPad, more and more companies have jumped on the tablet bandwagon, producing devices that claim to have better functionality for mobile computing.

RIM launched the PlayBook nine months after Apple's product was released. BlackBerry mobile handsets have traditionally been associated with the business market, and offer the most advanced email service available on a mobile device. Emails are delivered via RIM's servers rather than the network, browser pages are compressed by RIM and business applications are run on a BlackBerry server.

This adds an extra layer of security while offering an experience similar to that of working on a desktop computer, but on a smaller screen.

The BlackBerry PlayBook is also aimed at the business market – it has to be connected to your BlackBerry phone to receive emails and synchronise calendars and BlackBerry Messenger (BBM), for example – but RIM is hoping the tablet's more consumer-friendly features will broaden its appeal. Here we take a more in-depth look at the PlayBook.

SIZE AND SHAPE

The PlayBook feels a lot chunkier than the iPad 2. It's around 10mm thick, which is about the norm for a tablet, but it's not as wide as most of its rivals. It measures 130x194mm and weighs 400g, which is lighter than the iPad 2, which weighs just over 600g, while the HP TouchPad is a relatively hefty 740g.

The 7in touchscreen dominates the front of the PlayBook. A large, touch-sensitive area around the screen allows you to navigate using strokes and taps. RIM was one of the first companies to introduce a touch-sensitive surround, and the likes of HP, Acer and Samsung have since followed suit, integrating buttons or using the whole area, as on the PlayBook.

Also on the front of the PlayBook is a 3-megapixel camera for videoconferencing calls. Its image quality is far superior to the iPad 2's 640x480 VGA-resolution camera, and provides the closest experience to desktop videoconferencing available on a tablet thus far.

At the back, there's a 5-megapixel camera. This is also a higher resolution than the iPad 2's, but image

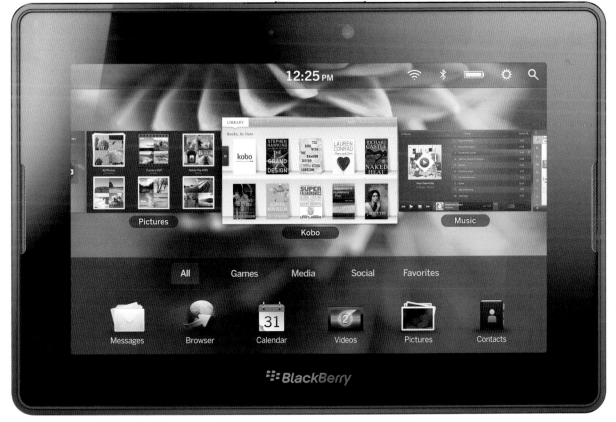

 425g

 5MP

 7h 13m

 5300mAh

 130mm

 Wi-Fi 802.11 a/b/g/n

 Networks TBC

 2.1+ EDR

 USB 2.0

 Email via Bridge

194mm

:::BlackBerry

The PlayBook

quality isn't just about resolution. The PlayBook's photos are quite noisy, but colours are representative. We're not sure how often you'd use the PlayBook as a camera, however.

To support the camera's capabilities, an HDMI port lets you connect the PlayBook to a TV to display images in high definition. You can even run two displays simultaneously, so if you're giving a PowerPoint presentation on a big screen from your tablet, for instance, you can display notes on the PlayBook itself.

HARDWARE SPECIFICATIONS

The PlayBook comes with a 1GHz ARM Cortex A9 dual-core processor and 1GB of RAM, a combination that makes working with multiple applications comfortable.

The tablet's OMAP4430 application processor from Texas Instruments features M-Shield mobile security technology, which helps protect content, transactions and network access – essential for a tablet aimed at business users, for whom security is vital.

RIM has also packed in OpenGL graphics support for high-quality gaming, and we were certainly impressed when we tested some of the latest fast-paced games on the tablet. This suggests that RIM may be eyeing the consumer market with this device as well as hoping to appeal to its traditional user base.

THE SCREEN

The PlayBook's 7-inch capacitive multitouch display may be smaller than the iPad 2's 9.7in screen, but with 1,024x600 pixels it actually boasts more dots per inch. Sure, it's hard to identify a single pixel on Apple's tablet, but it's even harder on the PlayBook.

The touchscreen on the PlayBook is also extremely responsive, which is clearly essential for a user interface designed to be controlled by strokes as well as pokes.

USER INTERFACE

The BlackBerry user interface has been completely overhauled for the PlayBook. It's based around active tiles in the task view, which displays the applications you have open on the homescreen. If you're playing a movie in the video application, for example, you'll see that video displaying on the tile. It will show any web pages you have open and, if you're working on a document, you'll see the actual document you're editing on the homescreen.

You navigate through the apps by swiping your finger, and tap to open them. To close an application you simply swipe it off the screen, in effect throwing it away. This element takes inspiration from the WebOS interface, and it works brilliantly.

Below the task view is a toolbar that shows all your unopened apps. You can cycle through this list by tapping on it or swiping your finger upwards.

You can change the order of the applications' shortcuts simply by tapping on the pencil icon and moving the apps around as you wish. Drag those you want to appear at the bottom of the homescreen to the top row; this is similar to the BlackBerry OS 6 way of doing things. To delete apps from your tablet, drag them to the recycle bin in edit mode. Tap the pencil icon again to get out of edit mode.

As previously mentioned, the bezel plays a major part in the PlayBook's navigation. Gestures across and up the bezel have different effects. For example, swiping your finger up from the bottom of the bezel to the screen will bring up the homescreen with the task menu. While you're in the web browser, swiping down from the top bezel on to the screen will make the tabs bar appear.

It's very intuitive to use, and quite unlike other operating systems. It's an innovative method of navigation, and has been implemented very efficiently.

BUSINESS FEATURES

RIM is known for producing high-class enterprise devices, and many of the PlayBook's features have been designed specifically for business use. These include enhanced security, push email, calendars and applications. However, email, calendars and BlackBerry Messenger will sync with your device only if you've connected your BlackBerry phone to the PlayBook. We'll go into more details about this a little later, but suffice to say that although it means increased security, it can a pain if your BlackBerry has run out of battery.

At the time of writing only a handful of companies had announced applications for the PlayBook. However, major players in the business market such as Citrix, Oracle, Cisco, Salesforce and IBM are all expected to develop software for the device.

BROWSER

The PlayBook's browser is one of its standout features. Unlike the iPad, it supports Flash, so you can view videos and other Flash-enabled content from within a browser page. Rather than sending you off to a third-party or standalone app to watch a YouTube fideo, for example, you simply tap the 'play' icon. You can also go straight to the YouTube website and watch videos from there. Streaming is speedy and clips play without any pauses or buffering.

Another browser highlight is tabs. These are displayed along the top of the screen when you pull down the top bar. You can switch between them as you wish, rather than having to head to a tabs screen as on many other tablet browsers. It's easy to add bookmarks or open a new tab at the top of the browser window; just tap the icons from the pull-down menu.

The browser has also been optimised for HTML 5, meaning you can do much than you can within the browsers on the iPad and other tablets.

VERDICT

For current BlackBerry users the PlayBook is the perfect large-screened companion, while its superb design, innovative features and simplicity of use are sure to make it appeal even to non-BlackBerry users.

BlackBerry

The PlayBook

From the front

1

MULTITASKING

All the apps you have open will display here as mini pages. They're live, so if you're playing a video, it will play here too.

2

CAMERA

The PlayBook's 3-megapixel front-facing camera makes it ideal for video calls and videoconferencing.

3

STATUS ICONS

The icons along the top show the Wi-Fi status, battery monitor, Bluetooth status, search and settings. Just tap on them for more information.

4

FAVOURITE SHORTCUTS

You can decide which of your applications you want to set as your favourites here. Just make sure they're the top row of icons when you open up the full menu.

5

SPEAKERS

The BlackBerry PlayBook features two speakers; in portrait mode, they're on the left and the right of the screen.

5

4

::: BlackBerry

The PlayBook

At the back

REAR PLATE

The PlayBook's rear is made of a soft touch material, with the BlackBerry logo in the centre of the tablet.

CAMERA

Around the back of the BlackBerry PlayBook, there's a 5-megapixel camera.

POWER BUTTON

This sits alongside the volume up and down buttons on the top of the device.

A sideways view

VOLUME BUTTON

The volume up/down key is on the top of the PlayBook.

HDMI AND USB PORT

You'll find the USB port and mini-HDMI port on the bottom.

So you've finally got your hands on a BlackBerry PlayBook – what now? Follow our step-by-step guide and you'll be up and running in no time

SETUP AND GO

Getting started with your PlayBook

O nce you've bought your BlackBerry PlayBook, chances are you'll want to turn it on and start using it straight away.

Setting up a new device can be quite daunting, especially if you're not familiar with the operating system or user interface, and you may feel a little overwhelmed when the welcome screen pops up on your new PlayBook. However, RIM has tried to make setup as simple as possible, with a wizard guiding new owners through the steps one at a time.

You'll need to follow these steps before you can get round to the exciting part – installing applications, playing games and browsing the internet.

When you first get your BlackBerry PlayBook home, it will need charging for a minimum of six hours. Doing this will ensure that the battery always operates at its optimum levels.

Once you've charged your PlayBook, you can get started. Over the next few pages we'll guide you through the process.

Setup and go

Setting up your PlayBook for the first time

When you turn on your BlackBerry PlayBook tablet for the first time, you'll be asked to go through the whole setup process. This may seem time-consuming and unnecessary, but it's the best way to get started.

You'll need to use a number of actions to navigate through the initial setup process. These are:
• Swiping from right to left on the screen in order to continue to the next step.
• Tapping the Back button to return to a previous screen.
• Tapping Skip to go past an optional step.

You should have already charged your PlayBook (see page 21), but if you haven't done so, plug it in now to ensure you have enough power to complete the setup process.

The first thing you'll see on your new device after pressing the power button is the welcome screen. This is a cheery hello from RIM.

You'll then be taken through the process to get your PlayBook up and running. A series of icons will appear, which allow you to set up each individual element of your PlayBook. We'll guide you through those features in this chapter.

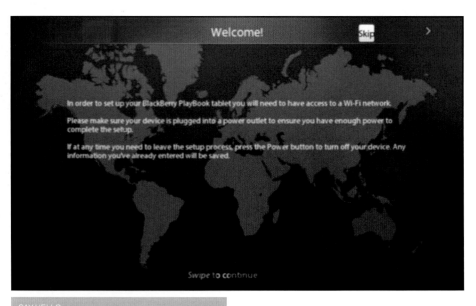

SAY HELLO
The first screen you'll see when you turn your PlayBook on is the Welcome screen. Swipe across the screen from right to left to continue

CONNECTING TO WI-FI

Wi-Fi is an integral part of your PlayBook, especially if you have the Wi-Fi-only version of the tablet. It's best to connect to your wireless network first as it will then make the other elements easier to set up.

First, ensure you're within range of your Wi-Fi signal and make a note of the name of the network and security key if necessary. A list of available networks will show when you go through the Wi-Fi set up manager. To connect to it, select your network and enter the password, if there is one.

You can also set up a network manually or connect to a Wi-Fi protected network. If you opt to set up a connection manually, you'll need to enter the name and password of your preferred network.

Once you've set this up, the PlayBook will automatically connect to this network whenever you're in range. If you want to set up an alternative connection, you can do so via the Settings menu.

Once you've set up your Wi-Fi connection, you'll be prompted to enter the date and time. Choose your region, and then set the date and time manually if it hasn't been configured automatically.

Your Playbook will now display the terms and conditions of use, which you have to accept before you can go any further. We recommend you read through these carefully before proceeding. If you don't accept this licence agreement, the PlayBook will turn itself off and you won't be able to use it until you accept them.

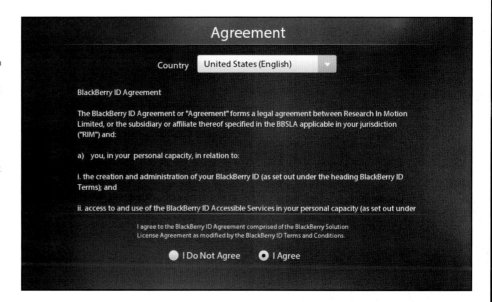

A TIME AND A PLACE
After setting up Wi-Fi on your PlayBook, you'll have to accept the terms and conditions in the licence agreement and change the date and time

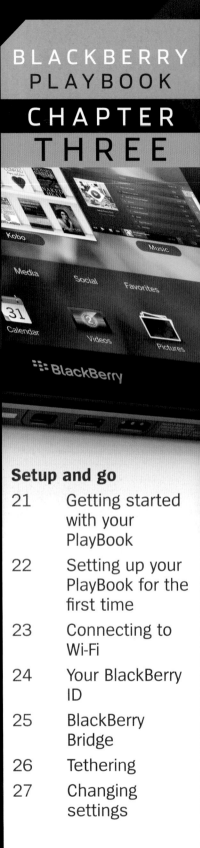

Setup and go

YOUR BLACKBERRY ID

The next step in setting up your PlayBook is to enter your BlackBerry user ID. This is similar to Apple's iTunes ID, and it allows you to access the whole range of BlackBerry services.

If you own a BlackBerry or you've used RIM's App World before, you'll have a BlackBerry ID already. If this is the case, simply enter your username along with your password when prompted.

If you don't have a BlackBerry ID, you'll need to set one up in order to download applications and use the full range of BlackBerry services. The process is simple; click on the Create a BlackBerry ID link at the bottom of the screen and you'll be guided through the process.

Once you've associated your BlackBerry ID with your new device, you'll be prompted to check for any updates to the BlackBerry PlayBook's operating system. This is vital in ensuring that your PlayBook runs as smoothly as possible. Many software or firmware updates iron out bugs and optimise the PlayBook for faster operation.

The tablet will automatically check for updates. If an update is available, you'll be prompted to download and install it.

Once you've updated the firmware, you can start setting it up with the server. This will enable you to send and receive emails on your PlayBook.

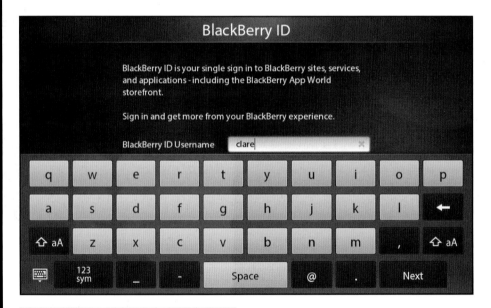

KNOW YOUR IDENTITY
You'll need a BlackBerry ID to download applications from App World. If you don't already have one, you can set one up here

SETTING UP YOUR BLACKBERRY PLAYBOOK WITH THE SERVER

Unlike traditional BlackBerry devices, the PlayBook doesn't require a connection to a BlackBerry server in order to operate. Instead, any connections to the BlackBerry server are made through your BlackBerry smartphone. You can do this by 'bridging' your handset with your PlayBook.

At the time of writing, it was uncertain whether BlackBerry Internet Service (BIS) or BlackBerry Enterprise Server (BES) connectivity will be available on the PlayBook. However, RIM has confirmed that native email, calendar and contact apps will be provided to customers via a future update.

GET UP TO DATE
Your PlayBook will automatically check for updates during the setup process

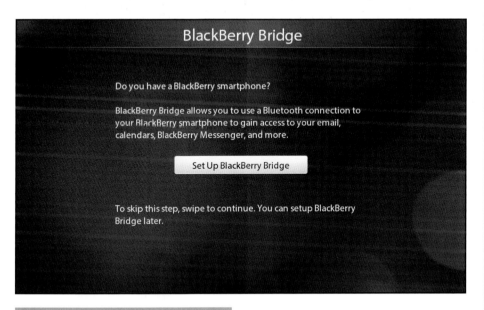

Software Update

Downloading Update

BlackBerry Tablet OS
Version 1.0.1.1710

0 MB of 267 MB (0%)

⚠ Your tablet will automatically restart to finish the installation

BlackBerry Bridge

Do you have a BlackBerry smartphone?

BlackBerry Bridge allows you to use a Bluetooth connection to your BlackBerry smartphone to gain access to your email, calendars, BlackBerry Messenger, and more.

Set Up BlackBerry Bridge

To skip this step, swipe to continue. You can setup BlackBerry Bridge later.

BLACKBERRY BRIDGE

As we discuss in more detail in Chapter 4, you have to set up a link between your PlayBook and BlackBerry phone if you want to use an Exchange email account, calendars or BlackBerry Messenger on your tablet.

One of the PlayBook's main advantages – particularly for business users – is that it's extremely secure when it comes to email. Only when both your handset and your tablet are connected can your Exchange email be synced to your PlayBook, along with calendars and your BlackBerry Messenger account. This is done using BlackBerry Bridge.

BlackBerry Bridge is simple to set up. We explain in more detail how to set up your BlackBerry with your PlayBook later on, but here's a brief guide:

1 Click Setup when prompted.
2 Turn on your BlackBerry smartphone's Bluetooth connection.
3 Download the BlackBerry Bridge application to your BlackBerry smartphone from App World.
4 Launch the app on your BlackBerry.
5 Scan the barcode on your PlayBook using your smartphone.
6 Accept for the two devices to connect.

The PlayBook will now go to the setup screen, where you can change all the settings and view tutorials.

TAKE IT TO THE BRIDGE
If you already have a BlackBerry, you can set up your PlayBook to synchronise emails, calendars and contacts between the two devices

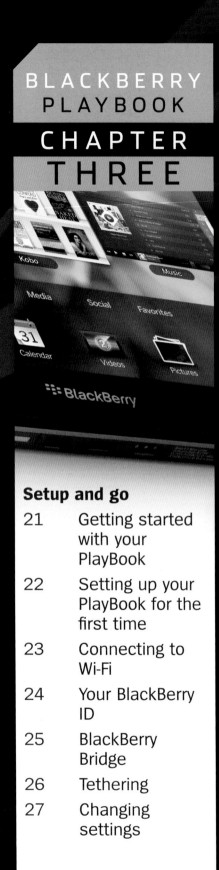

Setup and go

HOW TO SET UP TETHERING

The first PlayBook model will only feature only Wi-Fi connectivity, so you'll probably want to tether your BlackBerry PlayBook with your mobile phone. This will enable you to get online, even if you're nowhere near a Wi-Fi hotspot.

You can tether your Playbook with any smartphone, not just a BlackBerry, but both your network and your phone must support it. Android devices running on version 2.3 or later all support tethering, meaning you can get online in no time.

To tether your non-BlackBerry smartphone with your PlayBook, follow these instructions:

1 Switch on Bluetooth. It must be activated on both your PlayBook and your smartphone.

2 Pair the two devices using the Bluetooth menu on either device.

3 Tap the Settings icon on the status bar on the BlackBerry PlayBook.

4 Select Internet Tethering on the BlackBerry PlayBook, and choose Turn On.

5 Your PlayBook should now list all the available devices. Select the phone you want to pair with.

6 In the drop-down list, tap a service provider or tap Add and add a service provider to the list.

7 Tap the service provider and choose Connect.

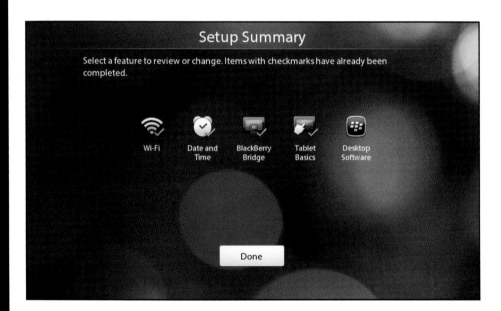

READY TO GO
Your PlayBook is now set up and ready to use. You can change the settings or set up further options by clicking the setup icon on the homescreen

BLACKBERRY TUTORIALS

Once you're up and running, it's a good idea to learn the basics of using your new tablet by watching the tutorials preloaded on the PlayBook. Much of the information in the tutorials is on how to navigate using the BlackBerry PlayBook's touchscreen.

To view the tutorials, tap the 'Learn about the home screen' and 'Learn how to access menus' icons. We've also provided a full guide in the Tips and Tricks section (page 66) of this book.

CHANGING SETTINGS AFTER YOU'VE SET UP YOUR PLAYBOOK

You can change your PlayBook's settings at any time by selecting the Settings menu from the home screen. This will take you to the same screens you were presented with when you completed the setup wizard.

Select Bridge to add a new BlackBerry to your PlayBook's bridged devices, or view the tutorials if you're not sure how to use a feature on the PlayBook. If you want to connect to a different Wi-Fi network, or search for one when your available Wi-Fi network isn't available, simply tap on the Wi-Fi status bar in the top right-hand corner of the screen. From here you can add a new network or search for other networks.

You can also enter the network name and password here if the network you're trying to join is hidden.

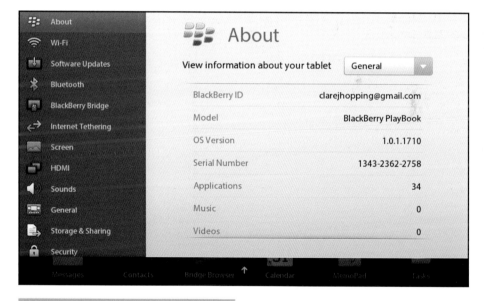

You'll need to introduce your PlayBook to your computer to synchronise your files and back up vital data. In this chapter we explain exactly how to do it

BLACKBERRY
PLAYBOOK

CHAPTER
FOUR

SYNCING

Synchronising your
PlayBook and PC

BlackBerry users tend to be loyal to their smartphones. Most can't bear to be parted from their trusted handsets for too long; they're essential for staying connected with the world, as well as for more fun activities such as taking snaps and updating Facebook and Twitter.

The same is likely to be true for BlackBerry PlayBook users, too. It's therefore important that linking your mobile devices to your desktop computers is as straightforward and hassle-free as possible. Your smartphone and tablet device should be able to synchronise key information with your computer quickly and easily so the whole experience feels seamless.

While data such as email will quickly download to your mobile phone over the air – either via Wi-Fi or the mobile network – and then to your PlayBook via BlackBerry Bridge (see chapter 5 for more on using Bridge), a significant chunk of information requires conventional syncing with your computer.

Tasks, memos, contacts and calendar entries will all appear in the same way on your PlayBook as they do on your desktop computer. You can also sync media such as music and videos with your tablet.

To synchronise the PlayBook with your computer, you'll need BlackBerry Desktop Software, which comes bundled with your tablet. Alternatively, you can download it from the BlackBerry website at http://uk.blackberry.com. The latest version of the software, 6.0, has had a complete overhaul of its interface and includes a number of new features.

As well as enabling you to customise your homescreen, BlackBerry Desktop Software also simplifies a number of key features. Backups, for example, can be performed with the minimum number of clicks, making errors less likely – and reducing the risk of losing valuable data.

First we'll look at some of the synchronisation basics that apply to BlackBerry smartphones before moving on to look at the PlayBook in more detail.

APPLICATIONS

BlackBerry Desktop Software provides a really simple way of keeping track of what applications are installed on your BlackBerry. Its easy-to-understand interface means you can see at a glance what your app line-up looks like, add and remove apps quickly and easily and keep abreast of updates.

To add, delete or update an app:

1 Once your BlackBerry is connected to your computer, click Applications.

2 To install an app (.alx) saved on your computer, select Import files.

3 To delete an app, select the 'x' icon next to the app's name.

4 To update an app, click on the '+' icon next to the app's name.

5 You can review your changes under Application Summary > Apply.

BACKUP AND RESTORE

You should always back up the data on your BlackBerry to ensure your files won't be irretrievably lost should disaster strike. BlackBerry Desktop Software makes both the backup and the restoring of data incredibly simple, so you can rest easy in the knowledge that all your contacts, documents, photos and other important files are safe.

To back up your data:

1 Once your BlackBerry is connected to your computer, click Device > Back up.

2 Click Full to back up all your smartphone's data or Quick to back up everything except emails. If you want greater control over what's backed up and what isn't, select the Custom option.

3 If you're backing up a smartphone that has built-in storage, tick the 'Files saved on my built-in media storage' box.

4 You can change name of the backup file, encrypt your data or save your settings using the File > Encrypt and 'Don't ask for these settings again' options.

5 Hit Back up and you're done.

To restore data:

1 Once your BlackBerry is connected to your computer, click Device > Restore.

2 Select the backup file containing the data you want to restore from the list that appears.

3 Click 'All device data and settings' to restore everything or 'Select device data and settings' to restore specific items.

4 If you're restoring data from a smartphone that has built-in storage, ensure the box 'Files saved on my built-in media storage' is ticked.

5 Enter the password if the file has been encrypted and locked.

6 Finally, click Restore. Note that files on the device will be deleted before the restore starts.

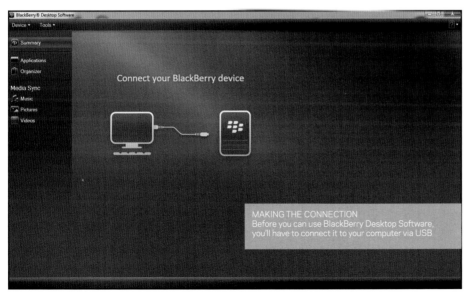

MAKING THE CONNECTION
Before you can use BlackBerry Desktop Software, you'll have to connect it to your computer via USB

Synchronising your
PlayBook and PC

SOFTWARE UPDATES

Users can be very demanding when it comes to software, and often have unrealistic expectations. Today's software offers amazing capabilities but, much like a car engine, it can need some occasional fine-tuning to run at its best.

That's where updates come in. When an update is available for BlackBerry Desktop Software, you'll be automatically alerted on the home screen. You then simply click the 'Update my device' button and follow the simple instructions.

SWITCHING DEVICES

Mobile phones are frequently lost or stolen, occasionally they stop working, and often an old phone will be upgraded to a newer model. Moving to a new handset may sound daunting when you consider all the contacts and other important information stored on your phone, but BlackBerry's Switch Device feature makes the process simple by transferring all your data and settings from your old BlackBerry to your new one.

To carry out the device switch operation:

1 Once your BlackBerry is connected to your computer, click Device > Switch Device.

2 Click the relevant device icon, then tick the Device data box to transfer your data and the Third-party applications box to transfer any compatible third-party apps, then click Next.

3 Ensure the new device is connected when prompted. Click on the device icon and your data will be transferred.

SYNCHRONISING

You can decide which information, such as contacts, calendar entries, memos and To Do lists, you transfer to and from your BlackBerry. You have complete control over what's synced, how it's synced and when.

To set up the synchronisation of Organizer data:

1 Once your BlackBerry is connected to your computer, click Organizer > Configure settings.

2 Select the tick box next to the Organizer app in the Intellisync setup window and click Setup.

3 Click on the Organizer app on your computer in the Available desktop applications list, then click Next > Provide synchronisation directions >Next > Finish.

4 Repeat the above steps to synchronise another Organizer app.

5 Once it's set up, simply select Organizer > Sync to synchronise the data.

MEDIA SYNCING

BlackBerry Desktop Software 6.0 comes with a Media Sync tool to ensure that your pictures and music are stored safely and accessible whenever you want.

Moving media files to and from your BlackBerry smartphone couldn't be easier with this latest version of BlackBerry's popular desktop syncing software. As well as giving you easy access to your favourite tunes and snaps, you can also share albums with your friends and loved ones, too.

Using Media Sync to create a playlist for your next gym trip or that big house-warming party is a simple process, over which you have complete control.

To synchronise your music:

1 Once your BlackBerry is connected to your computer, click Music.

2 You can synchronise playlists or song data by ticking the box next to the relevant item.

3 Select All music if you want to synchronise everything in your music library.

4 You can synchronise a random selection of music by ticking the box next to one or more playlists and selecting the Random Music option, then clicking Sync.

To synchronise pictures:

1 Once your BlackBerry is connected to your computer, click Pictures.

2 Select the Computer Pictures option, then tick the boxes beside the folders containing your images.

3 You can keep your pictures at their original size by selecting Optimize and unticking the box.

4 Click Sync, and you're done.

PLAYBOOK SYNCHRONISATION

We've shown you how to make sure your BlackBerry phone and computer are reading from the same hymn-sheet, and we'll now look at syncing your PlayBook with your computer.

MUSIC

Synchronising the music on your computer with your BlackBerry PlayBook means you'll be able to listen to your favourite tunes wherever you are, and transferring tracks couldn't be simpler.

To sync music from a computer to your PlayBook:

1 Ensure your PlayBook is connected to your computer.

2 Select Music in BlackBerry Desktop Software. AAC, MP3, WAV and WMA file types are supported.

3 If you want to synchronise specific playlists or genres or songs by particular artists, simply tick the box beside the playlists, artists or genres you want. To sync your entire music library, select the 'All music' option.

4 If you'd prefer to go for synchronisation of a random selection of what's left in your library outside your playlist groupings, just click on the Random Music tick box.

5 Click Sync and you're done.

PHOTOS

Much like music, you can make sure the photos that matter to you most are with you wherever you are by syncing the images on your computer with your BlackBerry PlayBook.

To synchronise photos from a computer to your PlayBook:

1 Ensure your PlayBook is connected to your computer.

2 Select the Pictures option in the BlackBerry Desktop Software application.

3 Select and click on the Computer Pictures tab. BMP, GIF, JPG and PNG files are all supported.

4 Select the tick box next to one or multiple picture folders.

5 If the pictures you want are in a folder that isn't listed, simply select Add folder, browse to the folder in question and click OK. You can then tick the box next to the newly added folder.

6 To keep your images the same size as the originals, untick the Optimize option.

7 Click Sync and you're done.

VIDEOS

The Playbook's 7-inch 1,024x600-pixel screen really helps bring videos to life, and again, syncing videos with BlackBerry Desktop Software is easy.

To synchronise videos from a computer to your PlayBook:

1 Ensure your PlayBook is connected to your computer.

2 Select the Videos option in the BlackBerry Desktop Software application.

3 Select and click on the Computer Videos tab. 3GP, 3GP2, AVI, ASF, F4V, M4A, M4V, MOV, MPEG-4 and WMV files are all supported. There's also support for MP4 for local video playback and video camera encoding.

4 Tick box next to one or more videos. If the videos you want aren't listed, select Add folder, browse to the folder in question and click OK. You can then tick the box next to the newly added folder.

5 To keep your videos in their original format, make sure the Convert Video box is checked.

6 Click Sync and you're done.

DATA SELECTION
You can choose to synchronise almost anything on your computer with your PlayBook

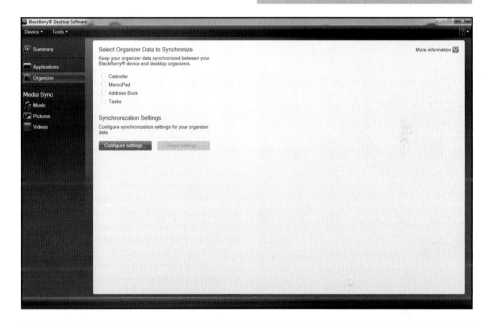

Syncing

Using your PlayBook on
Non-Windows
platforms

Although the preceding pages explain how to pair your BlackBerry smartphone or PlayBook with a Windows PC, you can also synchronise your data, music, photos and videos if you use a Mac or the Linux operating system. You may have to hunt around to find the right software and drivers, but otherwise the process is similar to the Windows platform.

Alongside the most up-to-date versions of Windows drivers and application software for BlackBerry devices, RIM also provides a version of Desktop Software for the Mac on its website at http://tinyurl.com/desksoftmac.

We look at using Desktop Software for the Mac in more detail on page 34. Here we'll take a brief look at some of the third-party Mac-compatible applications that have been written for BlackBerry.

However, some of you may use an alternative operating system, such as Linux.

At the time of writing, a backup and syncing solution has not yet been developed for alternative operating systems, although they do exist for BlackBerry smartphones.

Until software is developed to support the PlayBook, we suggest you use your Linux computer with your smartphone only, and then use BlackBerry Bridge files or a PC to view and transfer your data.

SYNCING WITH A LINUX PC

BlackBerry handsets can be synchronised with most popular Linux distributions, and if you simply want to move files between devices it's as easy as it is in Windows or on a Mac. For anything more advanced, however, you'll need to use dedicated Linux syncing software and do a bit of command-line work to pair your devices for the first time.

Two open-source projects, Barry and OpenSync, aim to provide BlackBerry users with more functionality than the ability to transfer data to and from a flash drive.

The Barry project (http://sourceforge.net/projects/barry) is "a GPL C++ library for interfacing with

BlackBerry handhelds". It comes with a command-line tool for exploring the device and a graphical user interface (GUI) for making quick backups. Its goal is to create a fully functional syncing mechanism on Linux.

Barry lets you explore, back up, restore and synchronise databases. However, some compiling is required, so you'll need to set aside some time to read the documentation and install the software.

Before you install Barry, you'll first need to install OpenSync, an independent project that can be found at http://tinyurl.com/opensync. Ensure you're using version 0.22 or later of OpenSync. Installation is straightforward if you follow the instructions carefully.

Once you've installed OpenSync you can move on to Barry, which is a little trickier. First, download the right package for your system from Sourceforge (www.sourceforge.net) or the OpenSUSE Build Service (OBS) page (http://tinyurl.com/opensusebs).

Sourceforge showcases packages for various Linux flavours. The current supported versions include:
• Ubuntu Gutsy Gibbon 7.10
• Ubuntu Hardy Heron 8.04
• Fedora Core 7
• Fedora Core 8
• Fedora Core 9
• OpenSUSE 10.2
• Debian Stable 4.0

On the OBS website, packages are located in sub-directories based on each individual Linux distribution. Be sure to select the correct platform – in particular, look out for whether you need the 32-bit or 64-bit version of the code.

Barry is divided into multiple binary packages. For example, if you want the GUI backup program, you'll also need the Barry library.

For non-development systems, you'll need:
• libbarry0
• barry-util

- barrybackup-gui
- barry-opensync (libopensync-plugin-barry on Debian systems)

For development systems, you'll also need the libbarry-dev package.

The Sourceforge site has a separate section for debugging packages, which will be needed only if you run into a problem that causes one of the above pieces of software to crash.

Finally, before you compile Barry, be sure to specify 'enable-opensync-plug-in', otherwise the compiled application won't work.

The first time you connect your BlackBerry and Linux PC with a USB cable, you may see a warning on your handset about there being insufficient USB power to charge it. Don't worry. You can make an adjustment using the btool command to correct this. Enter 'btool -h' via the command line for a complete list of options.

The GUI backup application included with Barry

is simple and effective. You get a small, easy-to-use display that shows the progress of the backup and which piece of information is being transferred.

The application also shows you the BlackBerry handset's device PIN (not to be confused with the security PIN for the SIM card). The device PIN is used for bonding a BlackBerry to a BES or BIS server and for connecting BlackBerry devices together via the BlackBerry Messenger application.

Type in 'barrybackup' at the command line and wait a second or two until it finds your device and displays its PIN number. When it does, click Save. You can edit the list of databases that the application will back up or restore by selecting Edit > Config from the Options menu.

Barry requires some basic knowledge of compiling software for Linux, so it's unlikely to be to everyone's taste. However, the finished article works and will give you basic backup and restore capabilities.

THAT SYNCING FEELING
There are a number of ways of synchronising your
BlackBerry smartphone with a non-Windows PC

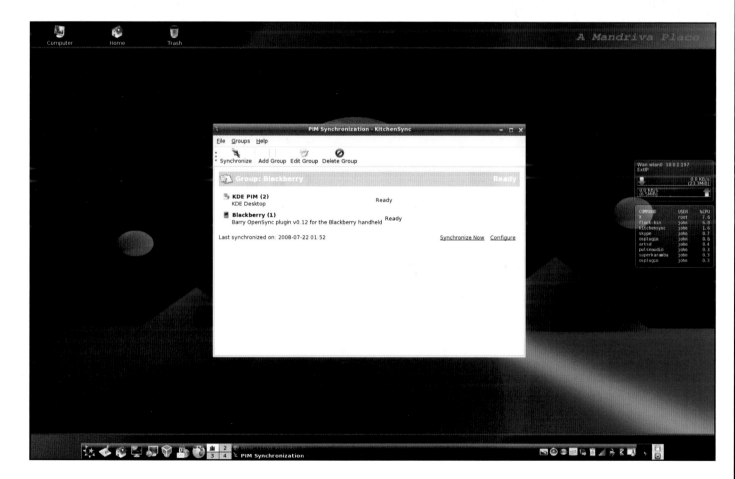

Synchronising your
PlayBook and Mac

As we've already mentioned, RIM's BlackBerry Desktop Software will soon be available for the Mac as well as the PC. Unsurprisingly, it will be just as simple to use on the Mac as it is on the PC.

BlackBerry Desktop Software for Mac is compatible only with devices running BlackBerry Device Software 4.2 or later, which will rule out many older devices. You'll also need Mac OS X 10.5.7 or higher, and have the relevant supported version of iTunes (which was version 7.7.1 or higher at the time of writing).

Once you've downloaded and installed Desktop Software for Mac, plug in your BlackBerry handset. The first time you use the software with your device, you'll need to go through the setup procedure.

On the first page that appears onscreen, enter your chosen name in the Device Name field. You can then select the synchronisation options you want to apply using the tick boxes next to the device's name, and choose where you want to save music if you choose to sync your phone with iTunes.

You can choose to synchronise all the data between your computer and BlackBerry device if you wish. Some devices can be synced wirelessly, so you don't have to plug it into your computer using a USB cable. If your device can connect 'over the air' like this, you won't need to use BlackBerry Desktop Software.

Before you start using Desktop Software, you'll have to turn on syncing services on your Mac. To do this,

IN SYNC
BlackBerry Desktop Software for Mac allows you to synchronise your PlayBook with music, video and applications on your Mac

open the iSync application from your Applications folder and go to Preferences, then select 'Enable syncing on this computer'.

ORGANIZER

To sync Organizer items with your Mac – and iCal events and other data on your Mac with Organizer – select the Information tab in BlackBerry Desktop Software. Here you can choose what information you'd like to sync using fields such as Calendars, Contacts, Notes and Tasks.

When you've made up your mind, simply click the Sync button and the two-way synchronisation will take place.

BACKUP AND RESTORE

To back up data to the default folder on your Mac, just click the Back Up icon at the top of your BlackBerry's screen or select the option in the main Device Settings menu at the top of your computer screen. Click 'All data' to save everything, or 'Selected data' to choose the specific data you want backed up. Tick box next to one or more databases and click Back Up.

To change where your data is saved to, go to the Preferences tab in BlackBerry Desktop Software. Choose the Backup Location option, click Change and type in the new path.

You can also schedule automatic backups. Click on Device Options, select the Backup tab and tick the 'Automatically back up when device is connected' option. Select an interval from the drop-down box and decide whether you want to back up all your device's data or exclude certain elements, such as calendars, from the backup.

To restore data to your device, you'll need to turn on mass storage mode. Mass storage mode allows you to drag and drop files from your PlayBook to your PC and vice versa. In effect it adds your PlayBook as an additional storage device, in the same way as if you were to plug in a digital camera, card reader or USB storage pen.

When you plug your PlayBook into your computer, it will ask you which mode you'd like to enter. There's a choice between mass storage and charging only. You'll need to ensure you choose the former to make any changes to your device.

Then click on the Restore icon at the top of the screen, select the relevant backup file and choose whether you want to restore all the data in the file or just a selection of it. If you want to restore only your contacts, for example, select that partition. Finally, click Restore to start the process.

Note that when you restore data to your phone, everything will be wiped from the handset before the backup file is restored, so make sure you do a full backup of all your data first.

INSTALLING APPLICATIONS

To install an application, go to the Applications tab at the top of the screen. You'll now see a list of available programs; simply tick the box next to the app you want to install on your device.

You can also install third-party applications you've downloaded to your computer. Click the + icon and select the .alx file for the app, then choose Open.

To make sure you have the most up-to-date versions of your installed software, go to the Applications tab and click on Check for Updates. If updates are available, you can opt to back up and restore your data while the updates are being installed or back up and restore the third-party applications. Click Start to begin the updating process.

To delete an application, go to the Applications tab and tick the ones you want to delete. Click Start to delete the applications.

MUSIC

You can also sync your PlayBook with your iTunes library using BlackBerry Desktop Software. Your iTunes playlists will be transferred, and podcasts and other audio files will be synchronised.

To sync your tablet with your music collection, select the Media section, then Music. You can choose to transfer your entire iTunes library by selecting All Songs and Playlists, or you can sync specific playlists by clicking Select Playlists and choosing the ones you want to transfer to your PlayBook.

You can add a random selection of music to fill up any remaining space on your device. These songs will appear in the Random playlist on your PlayBook when it's been synchronised.

Finally, click Sync and your music will appear on your PlayBook.

DELETING DATA FROM YOUR DEVICE

If you ever want to get rid of information from your device, make sure you first back up your whole phone to prevent losing vital data.

Connect your device to your computer and launch BlackBerry Desktop Software. On the Device menu, select Clear Data. You will now be given two options: All Data or Selected Data. For the latter option, select the items you'd like to delete.

To create a backup file for your device data, select Backup data before clearing the tick box. To encrypt the backup file, select the Encrypt backup file tick box. Type a password if required, click Clear and watch the data disappear.

LITTLE BLACK BOOK
You can synchronise your BlackBerry smartphone with contacts on your Mac and then access them on the PlayBook using the Bridge application

To use email, calendars and messaging on your PlayBook, you need to pair it with a BlackBerry smartphone. Fortunately, the process is simple, as we explain here

BRIDGING

Using Bridge to connect your
PlayBook and phone

Whether you're a business user or you simply intend to use your new tablet for personal stuff, you'll need to use a neat pairing app called Bridge if you want to use your PlayBook to access your mobile phone's calendaring, email and messaging functions.

Bridge enables you to access the core functions of your BlackBerry phone but on a larger screen. The two devices are connected using a Bluetooth connection rather than Wi-Fi.

Some people have complained about having to pair their BlackBerry smartphone and PlayBook, but it doesn't require much extra effort. What's more, there are benefits to be had from connecting your devices in this way; IT departments won't have yet another device to manage using BES, for example, as users will be able to access corporate data quickly and easily but in a secure fashion that complies with their company's existing IT policies.

Because Bridge uses Bluetooth to pair the devices, the connection is lost when the Bluetooth link is severed – either because it's been switched off manually or because you've moved out of range. The BlackBerry PlayBook has a typical range of around 10 metres when using Bluetooth.

Once you've disconnected your BlackBerry mobile and PlayBook, the data on the latter is wiped. This could be handy if you have a habit of leaving your tablet lying around and want information kept safe from prying eyes.

It's possible to access all applications running on the server via Bridge, including email, calendars, phonebook, BlackBerry Messenger and any files linked to your BlackBerry smartphone. However, the ability to access such apps natively on the PlayBook may be made available in the future. This would almost certainly boost sales of the PlayBook, as it will appeal to people who aren't already BlackBerry owners and those who want to use the device largely for entertainment and personal activities rather than work.

Fortunately, creating the perfect partnership between your BlackBerry smartphone and BlackBerry PlayBook is easy. Over the next few pages we'll show you how it's done.

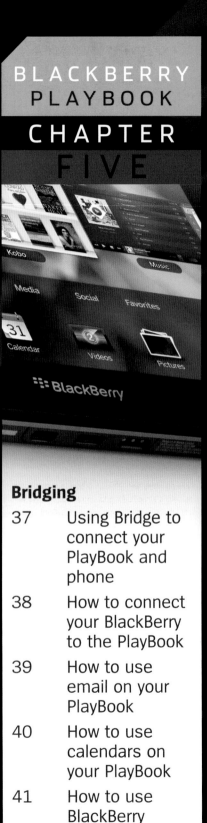

Bridging

How to connect your
BlackBerry to
the PlayBook

As outlined on the previous page, you can access, create and respond to emails using your PlayBook once you've paired it with your BlackBerry phone. You'll also be able to use BlackBerry Messenger (BBM – RIM's instant-messaging app) and calendaring and contact features on your PlayBook.

Before you can do all this, however, you have to introduce the two devices to one another. Only after they've been successfully paired can you start to take advantage of many of the core applications on your BlackBerry PlayBook.

Here we'll take a closer look at how to get your BlackBerry smartphone and PlayBook talking the same language when it comes to BBM, calendaring and email.

1 Make sure both your smartphone and PlayBook are turned on and placed close to one another so they're within Bluetooth-accessible range.

2 On your phone, go to BlackBerry App World and download the BlackBerry Bridge app.

3 Once you've successfully downloaded the Bridge app, install it on your smartphone. You can now introduce your two devices to each other.

4 Go to the Options menu in the top right-hand corner of your PlayBook's homescreen.

5 A 2D barcode will be displayed. You'll need to scan this with your BlackBerry just as you would if you were adding a new contact to BBM.

6 Once you've accessed, scanned and accepted the barcode, your BlackBerry and PlayBook will be connected via Bridge using Bluetooth.

7 If you now select the Bridge tab on your PlayBook it will display icons for BBM, Calendar and Messages, Files and Browser.

8 Simply tap on the icon for the app you want to use and you're away. You may see a message saying, "Loading your application, please wait…" while the app gets fired up.

9 In theory, you could share your PlayBook with friends and colleagues and disassociate your phone from the tablet then re-associate it each time you want to use the BBM, calendar and email functions. However, we would advise against this.

10 You'll have access to BBM, the calendar and your email account the whole time your PlayBook and BlackBerry are connected. Once the connection is severed, access to the app will also be lost. The data is then effectively wiped from the PlayBook until you reconnect it with your phone.

BlackBerry Bridge

1. On your smartphone, open BlackBerry AppWorld.

2. Press the menu key and click **Scan a Barcode**.

3. Point your smartphone at the barcode to scan it.

4. Click **Download** to install the BlackBerry Bridge application on your smartphone.

If you can't use the scan feature, in your BlackBerry smartphone browser, go to www.bbry.lv/BlackBerryBridge.

BlackBerry Bridge

Please enter a name for your tablet.

PlayBook-2883

Next

BRIDGE OVER UNTROUBLED WATERS
Connecting your phone to the PlayBook is simple: just scan in the QR code after downloading the Bridge app

How to use
Email on your PlayBook

Email has become a vital part of our working and personal lives. Such communication can help maintain friendships and business relationships, and we're increasingly demanding always-on access to our messages wherever we are.

BlackBerry users have a reputation for lovingly cradling their smartphones, sending emails and waiting for replies while in the pub, out shopping or lazing on the sofa watching TV.

You can access exactly the email functionality on your PlayBook as you can on your BlackBerry handset, but making use of the bigger screen and bigger keyboard on the tablet.

Setting up your email account on your PlayBook is easy thanks to Bridge. Here's how to do it.

1 Make sure you've associated your BlackBerry smartphone with your PlayBook using Bridge (see opposite for details of how to do this).
2 Go to the BlackBerry tab on your PlayBook's central menu display.
3 This menu will display a sub-menu, listing BlackBerry Messenger (BBM), Calendar and Messages, with icons for each feature next to their name.
4 Simply click on the Messages option to access your email.
5 Now, with the two devices tethered using Bridge, you can create, open, respond to, forward and delete emails on your PlayBook in the same way as you would on your BlackBerry smartphone.

Note that if you're typing an email on your BlackBerry or your PlayBook, the two devices won't mirror each other in real-time while you're typing. However, if you save a draft, read a message or reply to an email on your smartphone it will be mirrored on your PlayBook, and vice versa.

If someone sends you an presentation as an attachment, you can open it on your PlayBook to view the presentation in all its glory on the PlayBook's 7-inch 1,024x600-pixel screen rather than on a tiny mobile display.

Security is an important consideration in a corporate environment, so it's reassuring to know that no-one will be able access your emails through the PlayBook once the Bridge connection has been severed.

MESSAGE IN A BOTTLE
Your email application will display all your messages in a tablet format, so you don't miss any important news

TRUE TO TYPE
The PlayBook's large keyboard makes typing almost as easy as it is on a conventional desktop keyboard

Bridging

How to use
Calendars on your PlayBook

RIGHT ON TIME
The BlackBerry PlayBook can keep your diary up to date thanks to Exchange calendar syncing

Sometimes juggling the demands of work and our personal lives gets so complicated that we forget important meetings – or even worse, a family member's birthday, or your anniversary – or we end up trying to be in two places at the same time because we've double-booked ourselves.

That's why it's important to keep an up-to-date calendar that travels with you wherever you are. That's always been possible with a BlackBerry smartphone, but you can access all the same functions on your PlayBook – and because the PlayBook has a larger screen and keyboard, calendars displayed on the PlayBook are much easier to read.

Again, setting up calendaring on your BlackBerry PlayBook is simple.

1 Make sure you've associated your BlackBerry smartphone with your PlayBook using Bridge (see page 38).

2 Go to the Bridge tab on your PlayBook's central menu display.

3 This menu will display a sub-menu, listing BlackBerry Messenger (BBM), Calendar and Messages, with icons for each feature next to their name.

4 Simply click on Calendar to access your calendars and appointment information.

With the two devices tethered using Bridge, you will now be able to view and edit appointments, respond to and send invites and more in the same way on your PlayBook as you would on your BlackBerry smartphone. You can also view your calendar information in a variety of formats, such as day, week or month views, depending on your preferences.

If you're creating or responding to an invite on your BlackBerry or on your PlayBook, note that, as with email, the two devices won't mirror each other in real-time while you're typing. But if, for example, you accept a meeting request on your smartphone, it will instantly appear as a meeting in your calendar on your PlayBook. Similarly, if you edit an appointment on your PlayBook, once you've saved it your BlackBerry smartphone's calendar will automatically be updated, and vice versa.

If someone sends you an invite with an agenda, you can open the request on your PlayBook to see the details in all their glory. Simply tap the appointment on the calendar to blow up the details to check on the venue, time, attendees and so on.

As with emails, security is important, and like the email application your calendars and contact won't be accessible through the PlayBook once the Bridge connection has been terminated.

How to use
BlackBerry Messenger
on your PlayBook

There are millions of BlackBerry Messenger (BBM) users around the world, with more and more signing up each month, making it one of the most popular messaging apps around.

As well as being a great tool for colleagues to collaborate and share ideas, BBM is also ideal for more personal communications, such as keeping abreast of the latest gossip and staying in touch with distant family and friends.

PlayBook owners can take advantage of the same BBM functionality on their tablet. You can access the same features as you can on your smartphone, but will be able to see conversations better and respond quicker thanks to the larger screen and keyboard.

Using BBM on your BlackBerry PlayBook is a piece of cake. Before you start, make sure you've associated your BlackBerry smartphone with your PlayBook using Bridge (see page 38 for full details of how to do this).

1 Go to the Bridge tab on your PlayBook's central menu display.

2 This menu will display a sub-menu, listing BlackBerry Messenger (BBM), Calendar and Messages, with icons for each feature next to their name.

3 Click on the BBM icon. On firing the app up, you'll be greeted with a list of all your BBM contacts. You will now be able to send and receive

messages, manage your contacts and take part in conversations on your PlayBook just as you would on your BlackBerry smartphone.

Just as with the email and calendar features, messages on your BlackBerry phone and your PlayBook aren't synchronised with each other in real-time while you're typing. However, when you reply to a message on your smartphone, it will instantly appear as a sent BBM message in the conversation thread on your PlayBook, and vice versa.

As with email and calendaring, your BBM conversations and contacts are completely secure, with BBM becoming unavailable once your PlayBook no longer has a Bridge Bluetooth connection.

INSTANT MESSENGER
BlackBerry Messenger synchronises with your BlackBerry smartphone's contacts application

A tablet is only as useful as the software installed on it. In this chapter we look at what comes with the PlayBook and pick a few of our favourite third-party apps

APPLICATIONS

BlackBerry
App World

A s is the case with all smartphone and tablet platforms, applications are at the forefront of the appeal of the BlackBerry PlayBook.

BlackBerry apps have traditionally tended to be expensive and mainly targeted at business users, focusing on server-side applications such as accounting and customer relationship management (CRM) software. Now, however, a range of affordable apps, ranging from entertainment and games titles to business and productivity software, are available to download from BlackBerry App World.

Available for BlackBerry smartphones for some time, App World has been somewhat tweaked for the PlayBook. Although it's not yet as well developed as the BlackBerry smartphone version, it has the potential to provide all the software you could possibly need for your new tablet.

Downloading apps is straightforward. Open up the App World link from your homescreen and the featured apps will appear at the front of the store. Below these is a toolbar, where you can swap between categories that include the newest, top free, top purchased and recently updated applications. Switching between these categories will change the applications in the bottom toolbar.

You can also browse through the apps by tapping on the Categories link on the top toolbar. Many of the categories also have sub-categories and, although this can initially make finding an app a little time-consuming, it won't take long to find your way around. If you know what app you're looking for, you can search for it by typing the name into the search bar, also along the top toolbar.

The final tab at the top of the screen is My World, which displays all the apps you've downloaded. You can also delete apps from your PlayBook from here.You can view your apps by those installed, those you've uninstalled and those that are unavailable for whatever reason. If you've bought an app and deleted it, you can reinstall it from the uninstalled section.

As a relative latecomer to the scene, App World currently offers far fewer apps than rival stores. The number is growing every day, however. In this chapter we pick some of our favourite third-party apps currently available for the PlayBook, as well as looking at the pre-installed apps that come with the device.

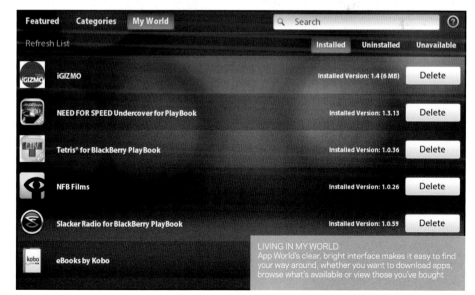

LIVING IN MY WORLD
App World's clear, bright interface makes it easy to find your way around, whether you want to download apps, browse what's available or view those you've bought

Applications

A guide to
Pre-installed apps

There are some apps you might expect to find on a tablet that aren't on the PlayBook, at least not yet: built-in email, calendar and contacts apps, for example. These have all been promised for a future software update, but initially you'll either have to use a webmail service such as Gmail or Hotmail in your web browser or connect to a BlackBerry handset with the Bridge software via a secure Bluetooth connection.

Bridge shows your email, calendar, tasks, memos and BBM conversations from your BlackBerry phone (as well as any intranet connections for your workplace) on the larger screen. You can put the phone away and work with the information on the larger screen, or keep hold of your mobile and use it as a keyboard for the PlayBook. Either way the information stays on the phone; the PlayBook shows you messages and contacts but doesn't copy them, so you don't have to worry about keeping two address books in sync.

You can use Bridge to access multiple BlackBerry handsets (although not at the same time), so you can share a PlayBook with the family and email and messages still stay private when you disconnect Bridge.

Bridge is separate from the Internet Tethering tool, even though that also connects to a BlackBerry handset via Bluetooth; Bridge works only with a BlackBerry smartphone, whereas tethering works with any Bluetooth-enabled mobile handset. Internet Tethering gets you online using the data connection on the phone when you can't use the built-in Wi-Fi.

BROWSER

The web browser on the PlayBook is based on WebKit and has Flash 10.1 support, so you can play Flash videos (such as those on YouTube) and Flash games. That means most websites and web apps will work in the same way as they would on a PC or Mac. Visit Facebook, for example, and you can use Facebook chat and games and upload photos and videos you've taken on the tablet (when you click the link to upload a photo, you'll see the PlayBook file browser, which lets you pick the file from your photos, movie and music folders).

HTML5 elements such as CSS3 and Canvas are also supported, so complicated page layouts and visual web applications will work well, and as sites that add new HTML5 features will continue to work properly on the PlayBook. It supports the latest web standards, such

as geolocation, so you'll be able to let the next wave of websites know where you are; ideal for getting maps or finding businesses without typing in an address.

The accelerometer support will need websites to write code specifically, but once they do you'll be able to play games by tilting or rotating the screen. Sites may also automatically reflow their layout when you turn the PlayBook to hold it in portrait view. It also supports the Video and Audio tags, so video and audio files embedded in web pages using HTML 5 will play directly.

You may see mobile-optimised pages on some sites; the browser user agent string tells web servers it's for a PlayBook or Mobile Safari, so sites can send simpler versions of pages that load more quickly.

PHOTOS, VIDEOS AND MUSIC

The Camera app enables you to take pictures or record videos using the 5-megapixel camera on the back of the PlayBook or the 3-megapixel camera on the front. The app controls let you change the zoom, pick 'scene modes' designed for close-ups or fast-moving sports shots and take 1080p video; there's even an option for photographing whiteboards in meetings.

Your photos are displayed in the Pictures app, which has a simple touch interface for viewing images. You can browse through thumbnails in an album or a filmstrip at the top of the screen, pinch to zoom in and swipe sideways to move to the next picture, or tap the Play arrow to view a slideshow.

The Video Player app works with H.264, MP4, WMV and DivX files, up to 1080p HD; you can watch onscreen or connect to another display via the micro-HDMI port; you can then either have the video playing on both screens or just the external display, so you can browse the web or play a game while you watch.

The built-in Music Player works with MP3, WMA, WAV and M4A (AAC) audio files. It has a nice clear interface for browsing through tracks by artist, album, genre or song, and you can also save multiple playlists. The controls at the bottom let you turn on shuffle and

repeat and change the volume, as well as control playback and view the details of the song currently being played. Music continues in the background when you switch to other apps as long as the Music Player is the default media player. If you install another media app and make it the default player, that app will have the background playback feature instead.

MUSIC STORE AND PODCASTS

The 7Digital music store, which sells around 13 million tracks, comes pre-installed on the PlayBook and has been redesigned with a new tablet interface. You can search for specific tracks or browse by genre, and scroll through new releases, best-sellers and featured albums from the front screen. Any music you buy is DRM-free, so you can copy it to your PC or BlackBerry and it will be stored in your 7Digital locker. A future update will enable you to see music you've bought on your BlackBerry smartphone, including via third-party apps that use the 7Digital store, such as Nobex Radio Companion, and sync tracks between devices.

The Podcast app lets you browse and search thousands of audio and video podcasts, including HD videos, from hundreds of channels and categories. You can store your favourites in the My Podcasts section, where you'll also be able to see podcasts you've downloaded and get the latest episodes automatically by subscribing. The Podcast app's player displays the volume, play, pause and skip controls onscreen.

EBOOKS

The PlayBook comes with the Kobo ebook reader and store. You can download out-of-copyright classics such as the Sherlock Holmes stories for free, or choose from over two million titles in the Kobo store. This stocks books by popular authors such as Bill Bryson, in genres ranging from cookbooks and popular science to mystery and romance.

When you're reading, the book layout is optimised for reading on the PlayBook in both landscape and portrait views. You can dim the screen, control the backlight and contrast or change the onscreen font.

As with the 7Digital music store, if you're already using Kobo on your BlackBerry mobile phone or another device, you'll be able to see the books you've already bought here.

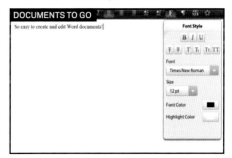

Applications

DOCUMENTS TO GO

This useful app lets you view, edit or create Word, Excel and PowerPoint files in its Word To Go, Sheet To Go and Slideshow To Go modules. This works with documents downloaded from the web or your webmail account, as well as email attachments received via Bridge (unless you connect to a company BES that has policies to stop you saving documents).

The large PlayBook screen makes viewing big spreadsheets or presentations more manageable, and means there's enough room for a toolbar with formatting options. You can switch between multiple sheets in a Sheet To Go workbook using the drop-down menu, and change the font, point size, colour and style of text in Word To Go. There are outline, notes and slide views in Slideshow To Go, so you can use it to create your presentation, and you can even use your PlayBook to give your presentation if you connect it to a screen via the micro-HDMI port.

For viewing PDFs you get the official Adobe Reader app for the PlayBook. As the whole PlayBook interface is built in Adobe's AIR, PDF support is good.

GAMES, UTILITIES AND MORE

The PlayBook comes with two games; Tetris and Need For Speed, both of which have been optimised for a touchscreen interface, allowing you to use gestures such as swiping to speed up your car during a race.

The built-in Weather app gives you forecasts from AccuWeather for your location, with a five-day prediction, hourly details and weather maps of the area. There's a clock application with alarms, too.

The Video Chat application is more like BlackBerry Messenger with video than a video-conferencing program. You can chat with any other PlayBook user over Wi-Fi using your BlackBerry ID (although you'll need to know their BlackBerry ID to make the call). There are no charges for using Video Chat, unless you're in a Wi-Fi hotspot that charges you. There's also a voice notes recorder, similar to the app on BlackBerry, for recording messages and reminders to yourself.

When you want to add to your collection of apps, head to App World. Here you can choose from a huge range of paid-for and free titles. Over the next few pages we've picked a few of our favourites…

MR BLUE SKY
View forecasts from around the world with the Weather app (above), and edit Excel files with Sheets To Go (right)

SPEED DEMON
Need For Speed (left) is fully optimised for the PlayBook, and more free games are available at App World (below)

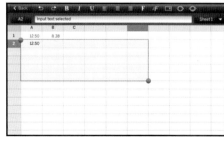

The best
Third-party apps

While the pre-installed apps on the PlayBook cover all the essential tasks, a wide range of third-party apps are also available. In time, the PlayBook will be capable of running Android as well as BlackBerry apps, and developers will be able to build apps directly for the underlying QNX OS, which will provide better performance in games. Initially, though, the first apps are built on top of Adobe AIR or HTML5.

Over the next few pages we've picked a selection of our favourite third-party apps. Bear in mind that the PlayBook's browser is so good that, unlike many other tablets, you probably won't need a special app for websites such as YouTube, Twitter and Facebook. All these apps are available through the App World store.

ADOBE CONNECT MOBILE

You don't need to fire up a PC to join an Adobe Connect video conference; this PlayBook app can connect you to a conference call by calling your phone, or you can use VoIP audio – either way, you don't need to type in a long conference code. As well as seeing the presenter you can use either the forward-facing camera on the PlayBook to send video of yourself or the rear-facing camera if you want to share what you can see. You can switch between the two cameras, which is handy if you're demonstrating something to the meeting.

The interface is laid out well for the large PlayBook screen. An overview shows you the presenter, the slides, PDF or desktop they're sharing, a list of everyone else in the meeting, public and private chat windows, a note window for questions and – if the presenter creates one – a survey in which you can vote. Tap on any of the windows and the app zooms in to show it full screen, so you can see the slides or watch the video and then go back to the overview or switch to asking a question or voting in the poll by tapping the navigation menu down the left-hand side. When you're in one of the individual windows, you get notifications for new messages in any of the public or private chats; just tap to go straight to the relevant window to reply.

If you don't have an Adobe Connect account, the app comes with a 30-day trial so you can try it out.

POYNT

Looking for a restaurant, a shop, a cinema, a locksmith? Poynt can help you find just about any kind of business nearby; you get the phone number, directions and a link to the website for more details. You can reserve a table at a restaurant, and if you're

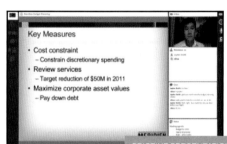

PRISTINE PRESENTATION
Adobe Connect lets you make video calls with friends and colleagues. You can even share presentations

LOCATION, LOCATION, LOCATION
Poynt helps you find exactly what you need, when you need it, whether it's a restaurant, locksmith or shop

BLACKBERRY PLAYBOOK
CHAPTER SIX

Applications

travelling in the US or Canada, you can find out where you can get the cheapest petrol, watch film trailers and book tickets from the PlayBook, then get directions to get you there. To help you decide what to do, you also get a current and a five-day weather forecast without leaving the app.

Poynt tells us you'll also be able to save the details of businesses in your BlackBerry address book and add reservations to your calendar, and if you miss a call from an unrecognised number you'll be able to use the app to look it up. One drawback is that you may need to change your location by hand; to do this, tap next to the Poynt logo in the top left.

WEATHEREYE HD

If you need more detail about the weather than what's provided by the built-in Weather app, WeatherEye HD from the Weather Network gives you weather reports and forecasts for multiple cities around the world.

You can choose between metric and imperial measurement units, set hourly updates, look up unusual weather conditions and view a wealth of other data, although there are no weather radar maps.

MAGAZINES

It isn't cheap, but the layout of Fortune magazine on the PlayBook looks great. You can jump directly to articles from the contents page or leaf through the magazine page by page. Reader's Digest and iGizmo magazines are both free to read and also look good on the PlayBook, although they have simpler layouts.

HUFFPOST NEWSGLIDE

Want to get the latest news in tablet format? The HuffPost NewsGlide app displays categories such as Business, Entertainment and Sports down the side, strips of stories across the screen and full-length stories you can swipe your way through without losing track of what else is going on.

The app has a very American feel, but if you like the mix of politics, entertainment, comedy, tech, business, sports, books and health the Huffington Post covers, this is a finger-friendly way of browsing through it.

NOBEX RADIO COMPANION

The PlayBook version of the excellent Nobex streaming internet radio app will enable you to listen to over 160,000 radio stations from around the world. Audio quality is superb, and we like the handy 'sleep timer', which you can set for anything between 15 minutes and two hours to use as a countdown (or indeed, to go to sleep with).

If you hear a song you like, you can buy the track straight away or you can mail yourself a link to buy it later. If you just catch the end of a track – or even if you see from the playlist that you just missed a song you'd like to hear – you can play a snippet to see if you like. You can also tweet or post Facebook links for your favourite songs and radio stations.

ISPEECH TRANSLATOR

Its interface is pretty basic, but iSpeech Translator is about more than just looks: simply type or speak a word or phrase and it will be translated into another language. Translations are displayed onscreen or spoken aloud in a human-sounding voice in 18 languages: Catalan, Danish, Dutch, English, Finnish, French, German, Italian, Japanese, Korean, Norwegian, Polish, Portuguese, Russian, Simplified Chinese, Spanish, Swedish and Chinese. You can also copy text to translate from the browser, email or other apps on your PlayBook.

You don't need to plug in a headset to say what you want translated; the app works well with the built-in microphone as long as you're in a fairly quiet room. The iSpeech Translator app is free, and if you're a developer you can also use it in your own apps.

LIVECYCLE MOBILE ES2

Adobe's LiveCycle workflow software is used by many companies to create electronic forms for submitting requests and obtaining approval for plans, expenses and budgets. Instead of filling in bits of paper or sending emails that can be easily mislaid, you can use the LiveCycle Mobile app for PlayBook to fill out approval requests or approve requests other people have sent to you.

RBSMARKETPLACE

If you need to stay on top of the Fixed Income, Commodity and Currency (FICC) markets and you have a corporate account with Royal Bank of Scotland, you can get the latest analyst reports from the bank right on your PlayBook as they're published.

RBSMarketplace sends notifications of new articles directly to your tablet, and you can take up to two weeks of reports offline with you. You can view summaries, organise articles to see what's popular or what fits your preferences, bookmark the ones you're interested in and then read the full report, look at the background of the analyst who wrote it and send them your feedback directly.

LOST WORLDS NATURE FILMS

The PlayBook's screen makes it ideal for watching movies, and the Lost Worlds Nature Films will help show it off to its full potential. This selection of full-length nature documentaries includes Ocean Voyagers,

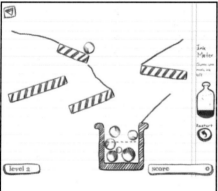

Ocean Oasis, Lost Worlds, Great North, Bears, Australia, Antarctica, Amazing Journeys, Alaska, Africa – The Serengeti and A Kingdom for the Dzanga Gorillas.

The image quality is great and the images are inspiring, but make sure you're online because you stream the videos rather than downloading them, which also means you can't fast-forward through them – just sit back and enjoy!

PLAY CREATOR

It's called the PlayBook, and now you can use it to make your own 'playbook': draw out tactics and play-by-plays for football, hockey, basketball and American football on the right background, with full and half-field layouts. You can drag and drop noughts and crosses to show players, draw in passes and moves and lock the screen so you can point at it without changing the view of the move you're trying to explain.

SCRIBBLE PAINT

The PlayBook's touchscreen enables you to do a lot more than simply type on a virtual keyboard. Scribble Paint turns your PlayBook into a blank page on which you can draw and paint. You can draw a map or a diagram and save it as a PNG file, jot down a quick reminder or amuse the kids with a game of hangman – the only limit is your imagination.

You can paint with a brush that gets thicker or thinner depending on how fast you move your finger. Other tools let you draw straight or curved lines, squares, rectangles, circles and ovals, and you can use the paint bucket to fill them with colour or spray-paint them with your finger.

DOODLE BLAST

Physics games are fun puzzles, and Doodle Blast is a very nice example of the genre, with a lovely hand-drawn look. You draw lines to indicate the path you want marbles to take so they bounce and roll safely to their destination. It's a very simple way of playing and is more immediate than the usual touchscreen method of selecting and dragging objects onscreen. Doodle Blast is an absorbing and rather addictive game that isn't quite as simple as you might think.

ARTGO COLORING

Need to keep the kids amused? With the ArtGO Coloring app you can create colouring book pages and hand your PlayBook over to let them colour in the animals and backgrounds using virtual crayons, markers and brushes.

You can create as many different pages as you want by dragging around the shapes to colour, save their favourites and even post them on Facebook.

ICONVERTER

What's 325° Fahrenheit in Celsius? How many inches is 24cm? Is my 20kg bag too heavy for an internal US flight? The 7in PlayBook screen means the calculator numbers in this handy converter for lengths, weights, volumes, area measures and temperatures are large and easy to press, making this a fast way to change imperial measurements to metric and vice versa.

FOURPLAY

There are more sophisticated Foursquare apps out there, but this app uses the PlayBook screen well to help you keep up with what your friends are doing. You can see photos of what might be of interest in a particular venue as well as upload your own, and see a list of who else is in the same place. When you find out where your friends are checking in, a map shows you their location so you can go and meet them.

BLUEPAD

You can create Word documents with the Documents To Go app, but sometimes all you need is a basic text file. BluePad is an easy-to-use and free text editor for creating simple text files on your PlayBook.

SHAREPLUS

Take Share Point with you on your PlayBook by syncing the lists and libraries you need using the SharePlus app. An offline sync runs in the background whenever you're connected so content is always up to date, and you can search the whole Share Point site when you're online, ordering and filtering lists by picking from the server-defined views you normally use, or search synced lists and sites offline.

Lists are displayed in a table or a grid to show details and metadata, and you can tap through for details, with pop-up dialogs for properties you can't see on a single line, and open documents full screen. You can read and edit documents, discussions, wiki pages and custom lists, edit and update lists – including calendars, tasks, pictures and contacts, as well as Office documents – and check files in and out to make sure only one person is working on a file at once. You can also save documents on your PlayBook to work with later, and change settings such as offline sync, background sync, the maximum downloadable document size and how to organise the list of synced files for each list you're working with.

SharePlus works with all recent versions of Share Point, including BPOS and Share Point Online, Share Point 2010 and Windows Share Point Services 3.0, through Windows or forms-based authentication, certificates or HTTPS/SSL, using your existing Share Point login – so your IT department won't complain

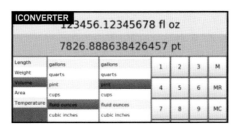

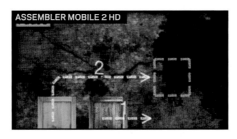

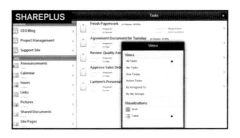

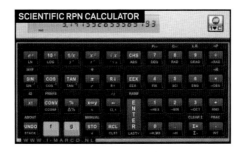

about you asking them to change things on the server or reduce security to make it work. All you need is the URL you usually use to connect to Share Point.

A Lite version is also available, and lets you view documents and lists but not sync or edit them. It's also handy for making sure you can connect to your Share Point site before you pay for the full version.

ASSEMBLER MOBILE 2 HD

This is another addictive game that can easily eat up an hour or two. Assembler looks simple: you drag blocks around and balance, prod, stack and swivel them into the right position to put the one block you want in the outlined spot. However, it gets more challenging the more you play.

The PlayBook version adds a new twist – literally. You use the accelerometer to change the gravity in the room you're playing. That means one slip and you have to start all over again, but you can also do some otherwise impossible balancing. For a free game, Assembler is exceptionally good.

SCREAMAGER

Turn your PlayBook into a scrolling sign with this fun free app. Screamager is ideal for attracting attention at events or finding the people you're picking up at the airport. You simply type in a message and then scroll it across the screen or animate it around the display in 16 bright and highly visible colours, which makes it look like a programmable dot-matrix screen. You can even scroll backwards or use reversed writing, for propping up inside your windscreen, for example, so people in front of you can read it as you drive along.

There are plenty of fun things you can do with this app, and it will also find a place in businesses and schools. You wouldn't buy a PlayBook just for Screamager, but once you have it you're sure to think of lots of situations when it could be useful.

SCIENTIFIC RPN CALCULATOR

Need to work hyperbolic functions in reverse polish notation? If you're a fan of scientific calculators such as Hewlett-Packard's classic HP1xC range, you'll love this full-screen numeric, trigonometric and statistical calculator with ten memory registers. It isn't an official emulator, but statistical functions such as linear regression, standard deviation, y-intercept and r, permutations mimic the HP models.

You can convert units with multiple properties, configure the scientific and engineering displays to your chosen precision, work with the unlimited stack and, most importantly – if this description is all Greek to you – work with the comprehensive help system to learn RPN and work with it.

Applications

SPIDER SOLITAIRE

Card games work particularly well on touchscreens, because the action you make with your hands is similar to moving real cards. If you like the Spider Solitaire that comes with Windows, you'll be impressed by this free version for the PlayBook.

You can play with one, two or all four suits, depending on how difficult you want the game to be. The aim is to uncover all the cards and place them in suits in ascending order from the ace up to the king. You can see hints for which cards you can move at any stage if you get stuck, although that won't always help you win!

ROCKET STORM

Blast away at the enemy rockets that threaten to overwhelm the solitary missile defender trying to save the base. We like the retro look of Rocket Storm, the nebula background and the gameplay. How long will you be able to survive?

NEBULA

Edgy music, psychedelic backgrounds and a mass of incoming asteroids you have to fire at to fend off or ricochet away before they hit your planet and shatter it – Nebula is a fast-moving game that manages to be fluid and almost hypnotic at the same time.

The gameplay is deceptively simple: you simply tap the screen to fire at incoming asteroids. You win points for deflecting them, get more points for pushing one asteroid out of the way so it pushes other asteroids aside, and a few extra points if you have any ammo left at the end. Add them up and choose whether you want to fire harder or faster next round – if you have a planet to keep defending!

BUBBLE BIRDS

We're surprised these birds aren't angry, given that people are shooing them out of the sky. Bubble Birds is a delightfully themed version of classic bubble-popping games, only with clouds of birds. Simply tap the screen to shoot three or more birds of the same colour. Chain together more birds of the same colour to get higher scores, especially if you can explode birds outside the main group.

The birds theme goes right through to the settings and high scores, which show up in a large cracked eggshell. The free version is supported by ads, and there's also an ad-free HD Premium version.

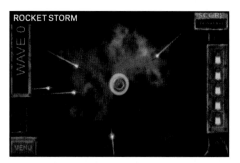

Developing for the PlayBook

The PlayBook is a very different device from RIM's BlackBerry smartphones. Built on top of the QNX micro-kernel operating system, it brings many familiar desktop concepts and development techniques to pocket devices.

QNX is a powerful tool, and there's a lot for developers to learn if they want to work with it directly. That's one of the main reasons why RIM has chosen the development strategy it has, initially restricting developers to high-level application tools – especially as any one of its number of PlayBook development options is equivalent to the whole development strategies of many of its competitors.

Eventually developers will be able to build PlayBook apps using several different techniques. Some applications will be built in Flash, using Adobe's AIR runtime. Others will use RIM's own WebWorks HTML5/CSS/JavaScript tools. You'll soon be able to package Android 2.3 applications and run them on PlayBook, as well as traditional Java BlackBerry applications.

The PlayBook will also get its own Java development tools for enterprise applications, while games developers will be able to use C and C++, along with OpenGL, to produce fast, powerful 3D games (and the same tools will be available to developers wanting to take advantage of all the power of PlayBook's dual-core processor and its accelerated graphics). You'll even be able to port POSIX-compliant UNIX applications to PlayBook.

With so many ways to build apps, it's not surprising that RIM is launching the PlayBook developer tools in stages. The first two options are already available, with AIR and WebWorks SDKs ready for download from the BlackBerry website. Android support will follow shortly, with the rest of the developer tools – including the native SDK for high performance applications and games – rolling out throughout 2011 and 2012.

RIM has developed a PlayBook simulator, a virtual machine running QNX with the PlayBook user interface, to help developers. It's not binary-compatible with the PlayBook – it's an x86 version of QNX – but it will run on most hypervisors, including the free VirtualBox and VMware Player. There's also a set of user interface guidelines, which we'd recommend you read before building your first application, as they detail the controls available and will help you design screens that take advantage of the PlayBook's capabilities.

Adobe's AIR is currently the main development platform for the PlayBook. Mixing Flash and HTML,

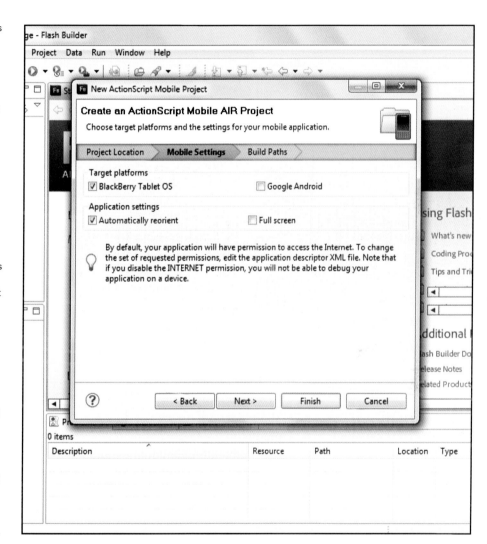

WALKING ON AIR
The BlackBerry PlayBook supports the Adobe AIR development environment

Applications

it's a universal runtime that lets you build applications that run cross-platform on everything from desktop computers (both Windows and Mac) to Android smartphones. Flash developers can use Flash Professional CS5 to take existing Flash movies and turn them into AIR applications, while more complex applications can be built using Flash Builder and Adobe's Flex application framework. RIM has worked with Adobe to provide extended support for the PlayBook in AIR, with access to the tablet's hardware and support for BlackBerry Tablet OS's look and feel.

You can download the PlayBook AIR SDK from http://tinyurl.com/playbookair. It's not the easiest of tools to set up, so make sure you download the Getting Started guide as well. We'd recommend using it with Adobe's Flash Builder 4.5 development platform. While it works standalone, installing the AIR SDK as a plugin simplifies development and lets you use the Flash Builder debugging tools with RIM's PlayBook simulator. RIM and Adobe provide a quick 'on the desktop' view for AIR applications, so you don't need to use the simulator to get started. This speeds up development time as you don't have to load and unload your code from the simulator each time you make a change.

Building an AIR PlayBook application is just like building any AIR application, and will be familiar if you've built Android Flash or AIR applications, as the PlayBook is designed to use the AIR 2.5 mobile device profile.

Start by creating a Flex Mobile Project in Flash Builder using the default SDK. You'll then need to choose to target the BlackBerry Tablet OS; this lets you access the PlayBook-specific features built into the AIR SDK. You'll have the option of building full-screen apps or apps that automatically reformat themselves as the PlayBook rotates.

RIM hasn't yet finished its visual editor for the AIR SDK, so you'll need to build application layouts by hand using Adobe's MXML language. It's not a complex language, as it describes page layout in much the same way as HTML. If you've handcoded HTML you'll be able to build the MXML for a PlayBook application, and if you know JavaScript it's not difficult to pick up Flash's ActionScript programming language.

There's support for working with remote objects, so you can connect to web services. That's important if you're building an application that links to existing line-of-business services, such as SAP or Share Point. You'll need to use techniques like this if you're going to make the PlayBook part of any business process or if you're aiming to use it to connect to online services with public APIs, such as Flickr and Google Maps.

AIR also supports database connections. You can

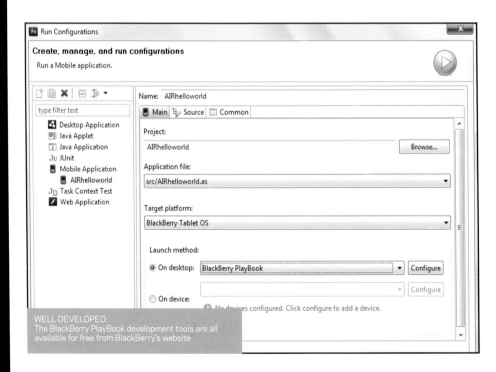

WELL DEVELOPED
The BlackBerry PlayBook development tools are all available for free from BlackBerry's website

use it with the PlayBook's local SQLite database, which can help support offline actions (especially important as the first PlayBooks will be Wi-Fi only). As well as the database, there's support for public shared objects and encrypted local storage for data that needs to be kept secure, plus a traditional file system.

It's important to manage the application state, as mobile apps can be interrupted in many different ways and your users will want to get back to what they were doing. Applications can be activated and deactivated by being pushed to and from the background, and you won't want to waste battery keeping them running.

You'll need to trap the appropriate events, saving and loading state so your users don't notice that the application hasn't been running. The BlackBerry Tablet OS will aggressively clean up memory, so watch for low memory events and save states even if the app is running in the background, so nothing is lost if your application is automatically shut down. You'll need to handle battery warnings similarly, and it's a good idea to include the PlayBook's battery-monitoring libraries in your applications.

BlackBerry Tablet OS's AIR support includes access to much of the PlayBook's hardware. There are API calls for the accelerometer, giving you 3D position information, so you can use the device camera and screen to give users a large-screen augmented reality experience. You can also read geolocation data.

It's a good idea to get to grips with RIM's extensions to AIR, which give you a library of PlayBook-specific classes, with support for RIM's payment APIs and for the familiar BlackBerry ID used by BlackBerry Messenger and the App World store. Other classes work with QNX features, including support for the PlayBook user interface, letting you use RIM's buttons, dialogs and controls in your applications rather than Adobe's default AIR look and feel.

The Tablet OS extensions also include low-level graphics and display features, helping you manage windows and handle scaling, which is important if your app will use touch gestures. Tablet applications are touch applications, and the PlayBook supports all the familiar gestures, such as swipe and pinch-to-zoom, as well as its own gestures that take advantage of the touch-enabled bezel around the screen.

Once you've developed an AIR application you'll be able to sign it with a digital signature and sell it through RIM's BlackBerry App World online store. Users will be able to download and install apps, and the App World application built into the PlayBook will keep them up to date with the latest versions of your software, as well as letting them upgrade from trial to full versions of your apps.

If AIR's not your forte, you can bring existing HTML, CSS and JavaScript web-development skills to the PlayBook. While its WebKit browser supports HTML 5 applications at desktop screen resolutions, there's also the option to build HTML 5 applications that work offline using the WebWorks SDK.

WebWorks applications are just like any other web application. If you've built one for the BlackBerry smartphone, there's not much difference when working with the PlayBook. You can build applications using your favourite web design tool, such as Adobe's Dreamweaver or Microsoft's Expression Web.

Once you've finished developing your code you can package all your assets into a WebWorks archive

and deliver it to users via RIM's BlackBerry App World. WebWorks applications can wrap existing websites, or they can be completely new applications custom-designed for the PlayBook.

The key to building a WebWorks app is the configuration document. This is an XML file that contains details of all the files used in your application, along with the icon users will see on their PlayBook, and the location of the initial HTML page to load. You can define the loading screen image your application will use, along with the transition effect that the PlayBook uses once the application has loaded.

You'll also use the configuration document to define the PlayBook API features your application will use. If you don't define the APIs you're using you won't be able to access them at all (it's the same for working with remote websites and services, which all need to be explicitly defined).

The PlayBook WebWorks API lets you interact with the tablet hardware, and with other applications. Once your applications are complete, you'll be able to compile them for distribution using the command-line WebWorks packager, which also allows you to give your applications a digital signature before uploading them to App World.

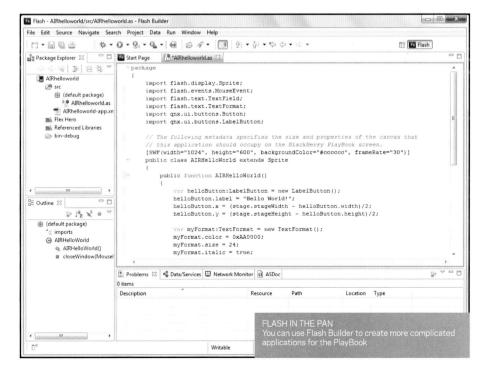

BlackBerry's reputation for mobile security is second to none - and the PlayBook is no different, so you can be sure your data is safe, wherever you are

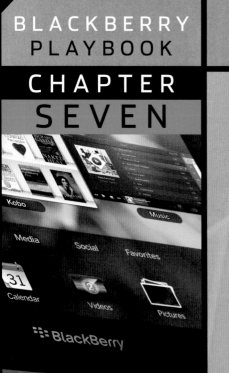

Keeping your data secure

RIM's BlackBerry smartphones have set the gold standard for mobile device security – and because of this they're used by police forces, governments around the world and even the President of the USA. It's a standard the PlayBook needs to meet if it's to be the enterprise tablet that RIM intends.

Like BlackBerry phones, the PlayBook has several different ways of storing your data, each with its own benefits and risks. You'll find the built-in tools and the apps you install all do things differently, and often they don't even tell you how your data is being handled. As a simple rule of thumb, though, you'll find that music, camera and video applications store data in a way that anyone can use it, while RIM's own BlackBerry productivity applications will keep your data as secure as possible. It's third-party apps that you'll need to be careful about, as you're unlikely to know how they'll treat your data.

The simplest and least secure option is the PlayBook's open file system, which apps can use to store photos, videos and audio recordings. The open file system makes it easy to load media on to the PlayBook, so you can quickly fill it up with music and video for entertainment on the road. There's no real security here, as it can be mounted over USB to transfer and synchronise media files, so anyone can plug a PlayBook into a PC and copy data to and from here, using the PlayBook like a USB drive. While this might seem a security hole, it's the same approach that RIM employs on its BlackBerry mobiles, using its desktop tools to sync media files with a PC.

If you're a developer using the PlayBook file system to store your application's files and data, you'll need to be aware that those files can be accessed by anyone using a PC. If you're writing an AIR application, one option for securing your data is to use tools such as the third-party AS3corelib encryption libraries to add file-encryption capabilities to the Flex framework. AS3cofrelib provides tools for working with the MD5 and SHA1 secure hash algorithms.

It's probably a lot easier, however, to use AIR's own secure storage features. These give you access to a per-application secure store, encrypted using your device password. While there's no explicit connection between stores, it is possible for applications being run by the same user to access each other's secure

WIPE THE SLATE CLEAN
You can delete all your data from the PlayBook in the Security settings. Just be sure to log out of your account first

stores, as the encryption is tied to the PlayBook user ID and password. It will keep data secure from user to user, but not application to application, so you're limited in what you can store. There are also size and performance limitations, with things slowing down if you're storing more than 10MB of data. It's possible to set a time-out for the encrypted store, locking it down if it's not been accessed recently.

The PlayBook also a built-in SQLite database. While it's not encrypted, each app gets its own database, and SQLite's architecture makes it hard to share

Security

databases between apps. And there's enough power in the PlayBook's dual-core processor to encrypt and decrypt data as you write it to, and read it from, the AIR SQLite store. It's not just AIR apps that get access to the PlayBook's database, though; there's also support for it from WebWorks HTML5 applications.

One useful feature is that RIM deletes any encryption keys that are stored on the PlayBook when you log out. This means that even if it were possible to copy data off a PlayBook, it would be very hard to decrypt it. Applications such as the PlayBook browser store save site credentials in an encrypted local store, and this approach means that other tablet users won't be able to access your saved passwords.

If you're worried about how PlayBook stores your email or contacts when you're using Bridge to connect your tablet to a BlackBerry smartphone, you can rest assured that it's as secure as your partnered BlackBerry. All the information you access over Bridge is held in a temporary encrypted store, with all your data removed from the PlayBook as soon as you disconnect from the BlackBerry.

This approach means that one PlayBook can be connected to a number of different BlackBerrys, ensuring that mail from one BlackBerry can't be accessed by another. It doesn't matter if you're using Bridge to connect to a BES-managed BlackBerry or one using the consumer BIS service – you'll get the same level of protection. As Bridge uses the BlackBerry device password, you'll be protected by any password rules set by your administrators, even though there's no direct control over the PlayBook.

The PlayBook's local cache of mail and contacts is encrypted using the AES 256 cryptographic algorithm, one of the strongest around. Each Bridge session generates a new cryptographic key, so even if data were kept on the PlayBook it would be unreadable in any other session, even with the same paired BlackBerry. RIM also uses AES 256 to lock down the Bluetooth connection between tablet and smartphone, using the same model as the BlackBerry smart card reader.

Like the local cache, the encrypted Bridge connection needs to be re-created from scratch each time you disconnect and reconnect, even if just for a moment. That means you'll need to type in your username and password each time you reconnect the PlayBook and BlackBerry; a small price to pay for strong security.

The high levels of security built into Bridge make the combination of PlayBook and BlackBerry smartphone one of the most secure methods possible for working with personal information on a large screen. AIR applications also get a secure store, and with support for multiple users, this is the first tablet you can share safely with friends and colleagues, giving them their own user names (and with their BlackBerrys, their own secure Bridge connections).

With plenty of memory and plenty of processing power, the PlayBook is able to give you several different approaches to securing your data, without compromising on performance.

HIDDEN CONNECTION
You can connect your BlackBerry smartphone quickly by selecting it from the Bridge menu

Passwords and PINs

Like all BlackBerry devices, the PlayBook is designed to be secure – and like the BlackBerry it uses a device password to handle security. It also takes advantage of the new BlackBerry ID service, tying a tablet to an email address and to an account with RIM's BlackBerry App World marketplace to handle application downloads and updates.

One of the first things you'll do when taking your PlayBook out the box is set up a BlackBerry ID. If you've already set one up (you'll probably have one if you've used App World on a BlackBerry smartphone), you can use it with your PlayBook. If you haven't, or you want to keep your PlayBook and BlackBerry accounts

separate, you'll be able to create a new BlackBerry ID on your tablet. All you need is a valid email address, a screen name and a password that's longer than six characters. You'll also need a simple password-recovery question in case you ever forget your BlackBerry ID password.

As well as your BlackBerry ID, you can set a separate device password. To do this, go to the security section of the Device settings and choose the password option. Slide the password control to the 'On' position and fill in the password fields. Once you've enabled a device password you'll need to enter it every time you turn on or wake your tablet.

It's a good idea to use a strong password with your PlayBook, ideally one that's over eight characters long and contains a mix of upper- and lower-case letters, numbers and punctuation. Like a smartphone, a tablet is an intensely personal device, and it will probably end up holding lots of potentially sensitive information that you don't want to share with the world – as well as applications that connect with your social networks and with your work. You don't want to lose your PlayBook, but if you do you want to know that your data is as secure as possible.

If you're going to share your PlayBook with other users, you'll definitely need a password. It's your username and password that handle access to any secure storage your apps are using and ensure that you're the only person who can use a specific paired BlackBerry over Bridge. PlayBook is designed to be a multi-user device, one you can share with colleagues and with family, so setting up a username and password is vital. Passwords aren't stored on the device between sessions, keeping your data secure when you're not logged in.

Your BlackBerry ID can be used as your username, and it's perhaps best thought of as a replacement for the BlackBerry smartphone's PIN. Instead of using PINs to send messages over BlackBerry Messenger, you'll use Blackberry IDs to connect over the PlayBook's built-in video-conferencing software. You'll also use your BlackBerry ID to download apps from the App World marketplace, tying your ID to credit cards or PayPal accounts to simplify the buying process. Owners of BlackBerry 6 devices will probably already have a BlackBerry ID, and it's a good idea to keep the same one for both devices.

You don't need a password to make the initial connection to BlackBerry Bridge, but you do need a BlackBerry with a camera. The PlayBook will display two QR codes: the first to download the Bridge software to the BlackBerry smartphone, the second to make the initial pairing between the devices. It's important the two devices make the initial connection this way, as it ensures that connections are trusted, meaning you won't need anything more than a password to make the connection between your PlayBook and BlackBerry in the future.

Although you'll use your BlackBerry ID for most purposes on a PlayBook, you'll use the device

DON'T BURN BRIDGES
You're taken through the Bridge setup process when you start your PlayBook for the first time

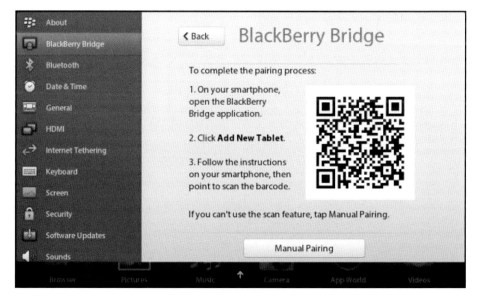

Security

password on your BlackBerry to connect to Bridge. A new version of the BES server software will include rules and policies for managing this connection, including controlling the strength of the password you're using. Even though it's passing over an encrypted Bluetooth connection, it's still important to have as strong a password as possible, as the information stored on your BlackBerry could well be sensitive, especially if you work in a regulated industry such as finance, the law or health.

Third-party apps can use a BlackBerry ID as secure credentials, either to unlock content and features or to manage application access. Developers have access to a set of BlackBerry ID APIs that they can use in their Flash applications, including tools for checking the status of App World purchases – something you'll need if you're a developer offering in-application purchasing over App World.

Some apps, such as the built-in 7digital music store, need their own passwords, and you'll set these up the first time you use them. It's a good idea not to use the same password for each application, and you may want to use a third-party password-management tool from App World to help you create and manage all your web and app passwords.

There's one place you'll still need a PIN, and that's if you're using BlackBerry Messenger through Bridge. As you're effectively cloning a paired BlackBerry smartphone on to your PlayBook, you'll use the BlackBerry's device PIN to set up and manage BBM connections, much as you would if you only had a phone. With Bridge you're simply using your PlayBook to get a larger view of your BlackBerry, so you'll be able to use familiar tools such as QR codes to handle making BBM connections, in much the same way as you would with a recent BlackBerry smartphone.

The PlayBook browser will help you manage your online passwords, with a secure store to keep them from session to session so you don't have to keep typing them in. You'll find this useful when working with webmail and social-networking sites.

PlayBook is for work and for play, and it needs to be secure. It's a very personal device, so it's important that you set up a good strong password as soon as you turn your PlayBook on for the first time. That way you'll know your data is safe and secure, wherever you and your tablet may be.

Secure network access

The PlayBook isn't an average consumer tablet. It's designed to work as well in the office as in the home, and that means working in some of the most tightly regulated environments around. Keeping your PlayBook secure is therefore vital, and that includes securing the data stored on the device and how it's transferred between tablet and servers.

RIM has already demonstrated an early prototype of a PlayBook-powered medical imaging tool for radiographers, which needs the highest security possible to ensure that confidential medical information doesn't leak. That level of security is important in many other scenarios, from mortgage calculations for financial advisers to handling case notes for lawyers, as well as in one of the BlackBerry's strongholds – police departments and law-enforcement agencies all around the world.

One option for secure network access from the PlayBook is BlackBerry Bridge. When connected to a BlackBerry smartphone you get access to its secure connection to a BES server and to the wider BlackBerry network. Bridge connects BlackBerry smartphones to PlayBooks using an encrypted Bluetooth connection. It's not a standard Bluetooth link, so you can only connect between Bridges – and setting up a pairing requires the two devices to be physically present.

Once paired, you'll be using AES 256 encryption to keep the link between the two devices secure. It's possible to move documents out of the secure Bridge environment using Documents 2 Go, so a future

AS SAFE AS HOUSES
You can access the internet securely on the PlayBook using VPN, and the HTML5 browser ensures all your PINs and passwords are kept safe from prying eyes

SECURITY BLANKET
Secure VPN connections allow you to access work files on the move. It's easy to set up a VPN profile – you'll find it in the Security settings menu

version of BES will include policies to stop documents from being saved on a PlayBook. Once connected over Bridge you'll get secure access to email and to the BlackBerry Messenger network, with the same levels of security you'd expect from a BlackBerry smartphone. Sessions aren't maintained, so you'll need to reconnect once you've logged out.

The simplest form of secure network access comes from the PlayBook's WebKit HTML5 web browser. With full support for web standards, this can work with secure SSL connections to web servers, keeping transactions secure. The PlayBook's powerful dual-core ARM processor means encrypted web connections won't be any slower, and sites won't need to fall back to open connections to maintain performance.

SSL is an important part of the modern web, and good SSL performance goes a long way to making sure you get the most from the secure web. WebKit also provides tools to show the quality of the digital certificates sites use to handle SSL encryption.

By building its browser on WebKit, RIM has made a commitment to deliver a high-quality HTML5 experience. Part of that is managing web passwords, which are stored for each user account in an encrypted area, so they're accessible only by the logged-in user.

More complex applications can take advantage of the security features built into the AIR platform used for most apps. Adobe's Flex SDK includes support for its open-source data connection protocol Blaze.DS. This binary protocol is considerably faster than using HTTPS, and can be used to build secure connections for line-of-business apps such as SAP and Oracle. If you're thinking of developing your own PlayBook apps that plug into company systems, you'll need to take advantage of technologies such as Blaze.DS, not only for secure connections, but also to give your users the best possible user experience.

PlayBooks are enterprise devices first and foremost, so it's not surprising that RIM has gone a long way to providing Virtual Private Network (VPN) support. VPNs make remote devices a secure extension of a corporate network, wherever they are. Good VPN support is important for devices such as the PlayBook, as they're typically 'third place' devices, used in coffee shops, hotel lobbies or anywhere you can get a network connection. But these places aren't the secure, managed environment of a corporate network.

PINS AND NEEDLES
You can use you existing PINs and passwords if you're shopping online or signing into Twitter

Security

They're insecure and untrusted, and are sometimes monitored by criminals armed with Wi-Fi sniffers. Connecting to a VPN provides a secure encrypted connection between a PlayBook and an endpoint somewhere inside a corporate network – either on a firewall, a security appliance or a server gateway within the network.

RIM has provided the PlayBook with a selection of different VPN clients, capable of connecting to most of the common network security tools. The list of clients supported at launch is:

• Check Point Software Technologies VPN-1
• Cisco VPN Concentrator 3000 Series
• Cisco Secure PIX Firewall VPN
• Cisco IOS with Easy VPN Server
• Cisco ASA
• Juniper VPN Series
• Microsoft IKEv2 VPN Server
• Generic IKEv2 VPN Server

Support for four different Cisco VPNs should mean that you'll be able to connect to most corporate networks from a PlayBook, and Microsoft's IPSEC VPN covers most other options. The generic VPN client should connect to most common VPN servers, including those built into SMB DSL routers. Setting up a secure

VPN can take some time, and often requires a lot of testing, but once in place will make it a lot easier for system administrators to trust remote connections.

It's easy enough to add a new VPN profile to a PlayBook. All you need to do is swipe down from the top of the screen to open the Settings tool. Tap on Security, then VPN to add a new VPN connection. You'll need to fill in a few details – including the address of the VPN endpoint and the passphrase used to make the connection – before you can connect. Each VPN connection you set up is saved as a separate profile, so choose the profile you want to use to connect to your corporate network.

RIM has given the PlayBook plenty of secure connection options, suitable for everything from casual connections to extending secure networks on to the device. Application developers can use secure SSL connections with WebWorks for HTML 5 applications, and AIR comes with tools for connecting applications to remote services. You'll also be able to use the BlackBerry Bridge tools to hook into the secure BlackBerry network, piggybacking on the BlackBerry data connection, which you can also take advantage of when tethering a PlayBook over Wi-FI to a BES-connected BlackBerry.

Wi-Fi security

The first PlayBook models released in the UK are Wi-Fi only, with 4G and 3G models coming later in 2011. That means you can only connect to the internet – and to enterprise networks – over Wi-Fi. With support for 802.11a/b/g/n connections, you'll be able to connect your PlayBook to virtually any wireless network, at home, in the office or in a cafe.

The PlayBook supports most common encrypted Wi-Fi connections, including WEP and WPA2. You're most likely to come across WPA – Wireless Protected Access – connections, and RIM has implemented support for both WPA-Personal and WPA-Enterprise, two different levels of encryption. Business networks are likely to use WPA-Enterprise, which uses a shared secret key to encrypt the connection. You'll be able to use the PlayBook's settings to manage passwords and passphrases, as well as controlling the networks to which your PlayBook will connect.

Connecting to a Wi-Fi network is simple. Touch the Wi-Fi icon on the PlayBook menu bar and slide the switch to 'On'. You'll see a list of open and closed wireless networks. Touch the network you want to use, and you'll then be prompted to type the network password if you're connecting to a closed network. If you're using a public Wi-Fi network you'll need to open a web page to authenticate, and possibly pay a fee before you can use the service. The PlayBook will automatically reconnect to networks you've previously used, much like the BlackBerry smartphone.

Initially there won't be support for authenticated Wi-Fi connections, so you won't be able to use either 801.X or Cisco's LEAF to manage connections to corporate networks. That's not as much of an issue as it could be, as managed wireless networks often use network card-based MAC address filtering to limit access to approved devices.

Other common network security options quarantine wireless devices such as tablets and smartphones, limiting access to network resources to extranet web content and authenticated VPN connections. RIM is planning to provide tools for managing security certificates with the upcoming native SDK, which will allow administrators to provision enterprise PlayBooks in advance, reducing the need for users to set up wireless connections manually.

The PlayBook's Wi-Fi tools will allow it to work as a standalone member of a wireless workgroup, sharing content with PCs that are running BlackBerry Desktop Software. You can walk into your home network with your PlayBook and it will automatically synchronise videos, pictures and music with a trusted PC. However, there's no option for direct wireless PlayBook-to-PlayBook connections, and if you want to share content between devices you'll need to use a third-party cloud service.

Applications can add their own security to Wi-Fi connections. If you're using the PlayBook's video chat application – which needs a Wi-Fi connection to operate – you'll only be able to connect to known BlackBerry IDs. That prevents ad hoc conversations with unknown users, reducing the risk of someone using your video camera remotely, and ensuring that you know the person you're talking to before you make the connection.

BETWEEN YOU AND ME
The PlayBook will allow you to join any network, whatever its security. Just keep that password safe!

Security

Security for
Developers

One of the PlayBook's strengths is the number of different ways developers can deliver apps. You can download apps built using Adobe AIR and RIM's own WebWorks HTML5 technologies, with native QNX applications and both BlackBerry and Android Java applications following later in the year.

That's good for end users, but also something RIM needs to consider in order to keep its reputation for platform security. Unlike other tablet manufacturers, who are developing their products in isolation and building on the heritage of desktop applications, RIM is using its BlackBerry experience to give the PlayBook a powerful and flexible framework for managing third-party apps and keeping your data secure.

The first line of defence in PlayBook's security model is App World. The BlackBerry online store certifies applications before making them public, running them through security tests and ensuring that applications aren't malware or inadvertently breaching security. As an additional security verification, apps are digitally signed by both RIM and the application developer.

Once in the App World marketplace, applications can be reviewed and rated, with apps that are perceived to violate user privacy and security quickly getting low ratings. It's a good idea to check ratings and read the application reviews before downloading or purchasing one.

If you have a BlackBerry smartphone you'll be familiar with how it handles application downloads. Install any BlackBerry application – either from App World or downloaded over the air from any website – and you'll be presented with a security warning that lists the permissions the application needs. You need to give the application those permissions explicitly; otherwise it won't have access to those functions. Tell it not to use a camera, and it won't be able to take photographs, for example; lock out GPS, and it won't know where you are. It's not like a PC, or any other mobile platform, where you simply install software without knowing what features it will use. Your PlayBook needs specific consent for applications to work.

With a proven security model, it's not surprising that installing third-party apps on the PlayBook is much like installing apps on BlackBerry smartphones. It's just as easy to download and install apps from App World. Things are a little different, however, in that application

permissions aren't granted at installation; instead you'll need to approve application access to device features the first time you run the app.

If you're a developer you'll need to declare explicitly which hardware features your application will be using. RIM has made many of these APIs restricted, and if you don't declare them and your users don't give permission, you won't be able to use them at all. Without permission they're locked, and your application won't run. The restricted APIs include GPS, the microphone and the camera, with the intent of protecting users from applications that hide malicious functions. After all, you don't want to be running a simple utility that's surreptitiously rifling through your file system or listening in to your conversations and sending data off to some unknown website.

RIM makes it easy for developers to add permissions to their apps, with a simple set of elements in the PlayBook default configuration file that all apps need. All you need to do is set the appropriate elements, and the restricted APIs will be opened once your users grant permission. There are no blanket permissions – you need to set a specific element for each restricted API you want to use.

There's a lot you can manage, and the available elements and services are easy to define, controlling a mix of native and Flash APIs:

access_internet: Set this for any application that needs to access a remote resource using a network connection. This opens up all the networking APIs.
access_shared: Set this for any application that needs to access the shared file system. This opens up the flash.net.SharedObject, flash.filesystem.FileStream and flash.filesystem.File APIs.
play_audio: Set this for any application that needs to use the PlayBook's audio controls. This opens up the qnx.media.MediaControl and flash.media.Sound APIs.
read_geolocation: Set this for any application that needs to know the location of the PlayBook, whether it's for mapping or for location-sensitive advertising. This opens up the flash.sensors.Geolocation API.
record_audio: This allows your applications to access the audio stream from the microphone. It opens up the flash.media.Microphone API.
set_audio_volume: If your applications need to manage audio volume, then you'll need to set this

PERMISSION TO LAND
You can adjust the permission details for all your apps via the Security settings

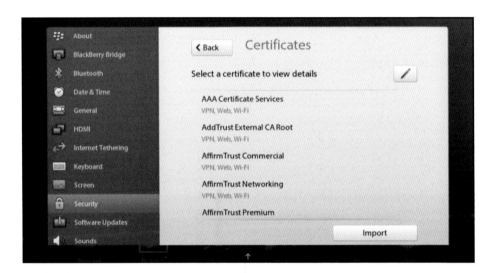

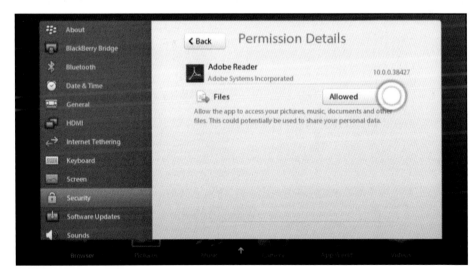

to access the volume control. This opens up the qnx.media.MediaControl API.

use_camera: The PlayBook has two cameras, one at the front and one at the rear. If your application needs to access data from one or more cameras, then you need to enable this permission. This opens up the flash.media.Camera API.

This approach is very different from the one taken by traditional AIR or Flash applications, as features you may have taken for granted in the standard Flash APIs are restricted by the PlayBook's security model. You'll need to take this into account if you're porting an existing AIR or Flash application to the PlayBook.

Setting the permission requests is easy enough. All you need to do is choose the permissions you want to use and then include them in the default blackberry-tablet.xml file. The following sample file is for an augmented reality game that needs to use the camera, know where you are and access game resources on the internet.

```
<qnx>
  <icon>
    <image>my_application.png</image>
  </icon>
  <publisher>Big Software Company</publisher>
  <category>core.games</category>
  <splashscreen>loading_screen.jpg</
    splashscreen>
  <permission>use_camera</permission>
  <permission>read_geolocation</permission>
  <permission>play_audio</permission>
  <permission>access_internet</permission>
</qnx>
```

As WebWorks uses higher-level APIs than AIR, fewer permissions are needed. However, you'll still need users to give permission for access to local data and for camera and location data. You'll also need to add specific permissions for any external websites or services, either giving external sites access to PlayBook APIs or only loading content, blocking them from using the built-in device features. You can control which features external sites can access, and if your application works with more than one site, each site can be given its own set of features.

We expose some of the PlayBook's hidden features and reveal the time-saving tips that will help you make the most of your device

TIPS AND TRICKS

CHAPTER EIGHT

Managing attachments

Email is a core part of our everyday lives, both at work and play, and email-equipped smartphones have become a trusted companion, keeping us connected at all times wherever we are.

The content of an email is usually what matters most, but it's also important that your phone or tablet device can deal with the attachments that often accompany a message.

You'll be pleased to hear that accessing emails and attachments is easy on the BlackBerry PlayBook. When you receive an email on your BlackBerry smartphone, if you're connected via Bridge you can simply tap on the attachment and it will download. The preinstalled Documents To Go app will then make sense of the attachment.

A word of caution, though. Many viruses are transmitted through attachments, which can spell bad news if they're not handled properly. Just as on a desktop PC, you should open attachments on your mobile devices only from trusted sources in case they contain something harmful.

If you're using BES, you get an extra level of protection as attachments will be encrypted using the same type of security used for your corporate emails.

There's a bit of a learning curve involved in teaching your BlackBerry how best to handle attachments, which you'll need to know if you plan to connect your BlackBerry to your PlayBook. Thankfully, though, it's top of the class when it comes to learning.

You'll have no problem viewing the body copy of emails. You'll be told the name of any attachments, their file type and size. That's as much as your BlackBerry will share with you until you tell it otherwise.

To see what you're dealing with, you have to choose to download the attachment, but you don't necessarily have to open it. You can opt to open everything or view a table of contents to help you make up your mind as to your next move. You may need to install the BlackBerry attachment application so the device

is aware of what policies and procedures to follow when it encounters an attachment.

According to the BlackBerry website, you can open any of the following file types, even if they've been compressed into the .zip format:
• Microsoft Office Excel, PowerPoint and Word files
• Corel WordPerfect files
• Adobe PDF files
• ASCII documents
• HTML attachments
• JPG, BMP, GIF, PNG and TIFF images.

In the desktop or laptop world, your computer's performance is affected by how much you've downloaded, as well as what you're actually doing. Downloading attachments can have the same effect on how your handset functions.

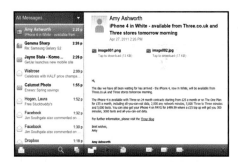

NO STRINGS ATTACHED
Just tap on the attachment icon in the email message and it will open instantly

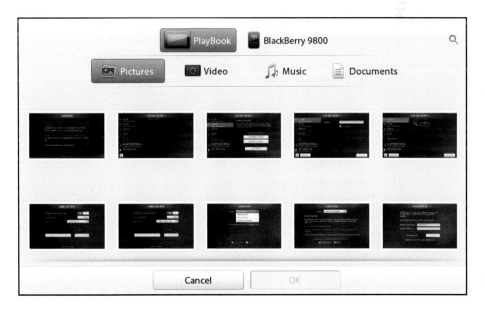

Tips and tricks

Multitasking

O ne of the major advantages of the BlackBerry PlayBook is its ability to perform more than one task at a time. This is a tablet that has the brains and the power to demonstrate true multitasking in action.

Whether you need to switch between business applications or quickly go back to work mode when the boss walks into the office while you're in the middle of a game, the PlayBook's multitasking capabilities make opening and working in more than one app simultaneously a painless process.

HOW TO ACCESS AND SWITCH APPS

You can quickly and easily open more than one app at a time. Here's how:

1 Open an application by selecting it from the menu or the shortcut toolbar at the bottom of the screen.

2 Once the application has opened, you can switch back to the homescreen by pulling up from below the display (starting at the touch-sensitive surround) to the centre of the screen.

3 The open application will show as a 'card' in the centre of the homescreen.

4 Select the other application you want to open from the menu or the bottom toolbar.

5 Once the second application has opened, you can switch between the two apps by pulling up the bottom toolbar to go back to the homescreen or swiping to the left or the ight across the screen.

ALL TOGETHER NOW
Multitasking is easy on the PlayBook: just swipe up from any application and you'll be taken to the homescreen, displaying all the open apps in live view

Gestures and navigation

Once you've set up your PlayBook, you have the option to view the tutorials that come with the device. It's useful to take a look at these before you start using your PlayBook if you're not familiar with its interface, because different gestures and different taps do different things.

Here's a guide of the most commonly used gestures to get you started.

SWIPING

As is the case with many tablets and touchscreen devices, the best way to get around is to swipe across the screen. Swiping to the side allows you to navigate through your homescreens, as well as the different menus and shortcuts.

If you're presented with a list or multiple icons, you can swipe up and down to scroll through them. Keeping your finger on the screen while swiping will control the scrolling, while flicking up and down with your finger will make the scrolling faster but give you less control. This is the best way to navigate quickly.

You'll sometimes need to swipe a little slower or use shorter swipes on the screen. This is especially useful if you want to bring up the homescreen when you're in an app or you want to pull the menu bar down when you're in the browser or gallery.

Swiping also comes in handy when you want to switch between apps without going back to the homescreen. If you have an app open, just swipe to the left or the right, from the screen to the surround, to switch between applications without returning to the main menu.

PINCHING

Pinching is another gesture you may be familiar with if you've used a touchscreen device in the past. It's used for zooming in and out of web pages, photos and documents.

To zoom in, you 'open pinch'. This means you start with your thumb and forefinger together and then spread them apart while touching the screen. If you

want to zoom out, you pinch your fingers together again on the screen.

DRAGGING

The BlackBerry PlayBook has an intuitive interface that allows you to move files, folders and chunks of text simply by dragging them around. For example, if you want to move one of your photos from one folder to another, just press and hold it, then move it to the new location.

The same technique can be used to move applications around and change your favourites. If you have the Task Manager open, you can drag the applications around to change the priority. If you want to switch an open web page with your email inbox, for example, just drag the web page card so it's in front of the email card.

SWITCH AND SWIPE
The BlackBerry PlayBook can be controlled with a series of swipes, using the screen surround as your starting point

BlackBerry

Tips and tricks

Keyboard shortcuts

If you're a seasoned BlackBerry user, you'll already know how much time they can save you. The PlayBook will build on this solid foundation, helping you get the most out of your time, whether you're at work, at home or out and about.

To speed things up even more, you can also \use a range of keyboard shortcuts to open apps, send messages quickly and more. We've already mentioned some of the PlayBook's time-saving features, such as gestures and multitasking, but here's a rundown of the keyboard shortcuts for BlackBerry smartphones.

MESSAGING SHORTCUTS
These shortcuts can be used in a message

DESIRED ACTION	SHORTCUT
REPLY TO A MESSAGE	PRESS R
REPLY TO ALL	PRESS L
FORWARD MESSAGE	PRESS F
FILE HIGHLIGHTED EMAIL MESSAGE	PRESS I
VIEW EMAIL ADDRESS OF A CONTACT IN A MESSAGE	HIGHLIGHT THE CONTACT AND PRESS Q. TO VIEW THE DISPLAY NAME AGAIN, PRESS Q

Shortcuts that can be used in a message list

DESIRED ACTION	SHORTCUT
OPEN A HIGHLIGHTED MESSAGE	PRESS ENTER
COMPOSE MESSAGE FROM THE MESSAGE LIST	PRESS C
MARK A MESSAGE AS OPENED OR UNOPENED	PRESS ALT AND U
VIEW RECEIVED MESSAGES	PRESS ALT AND I
VIEW SENT MESSAGES	PRESS ALT AND O
VIEW VOICEMAIL MESSAGES	PRESS ALT AND V
VIEW SHORT MESSAGE SERVICE (SMS) TEXTS	PRESS ALT AND S
VIEW CALL LOGS	PRESS ALT AND P
VIEW ALL YOUR MESSAGES AGAIN	PRESS THE ESCAPE/ BACK KEY

Shortcuts for moving around a message list

DESIRED ACTION	SHORTCUT
MOVE TO TOP OF SCREEN	PRESS SHIFT KEY AND SPACE
MOVE TO BOTTOM OF SCREEN	PRESS SPACE
MOVE TO TOP OF MESSAGE LIST	PRESS T
MOVE TO BOTTOM OF MESSAGE LIST	PRESS B
MOVE TO NEXT DATE	PRESS N
MOVE TO PREVIOUS DATE	PRESS P
MOVE TO NEXT UNOPENED ITEM	PRESS U
MOVE TO NEXT RELATED MESSAGE	PRESS J
MOVE TO PREVIOUS RELATED MESSAGE	PRESS K

BLACKBERRY USE MADE EASY

These built-in shortcuts are often missed by users, despite being in the manual

DESIRED ACTION	SHORTCUT
INSERT A FULL STOP	PRESS SPACE KEY TWICE
INSERT @ AND FULLSTOPS IN EMAIL ADDRESSES	PRESS 'SPACE' KEY WHILE TYPING IN THE ADDRESS
TYPE AN ACCENT OR SPECIAL CHARACTER	HOLD THE APPROPRIATE LETTER KEY AND ROLL THE TRACKBALL OR TRACK PAD
CAPITALISE A LETTER	HOLD THE LETTER KEY UNTIL THE CAPITALISED VERSION APPEARS
EXIT A SCREEN OR DIALOG BOX	PRESS ESCAPE/BACK BUTTON
MOVE THE CURSOR IN A DIFFERENT DIRECTION	PRESS ALT KEY AND ROLL THE TRACKBALL OR PAD
CHANGE AN OPTION FIELD	HOLD ALT KEY AND CLICK A VALUE
MOVE TO AN ITEM IN A LIST OR MENU	PRESS THE FIRST LETTER OF THE ITEM
SELECT A TICK BOX	PRESS SPACE KEY. TO CLEAR THE BOX, PRESS SPACE KEY AGAIN
SELECT A LINE OF TEXT	PRESS SHIFT AND ROLL THE TRACKBALL OR OPTICAL PAD
TURN ON THE BACKLIGHTING	PRESS (BUT DON'T HOLD) POWER BUTTON
FIND CONTACTS FROM THE BLACKBERRY HOMESCREEN	PRESS THE LETTER KEYS FOR THE CONTACT'S FIRST AND LAST INITIALS WITH A SPACE BETWEEN THEM
SWITCH TO ANOTHER PROGRAM	HOLD DOWN THE BLACKBERRY BUTTON UNTIL THE PROGRAMS APPEAR. TOGGLE THROUGH THEM USING THE TRACKBALL OR PAD AND CLICK ENTER TO SELECT
MOVE DOWN A SCREEN	PRESS SPACE KEY
MOVE UP A SCREEN	PRESS SHIFT KEY PLUS SPACE KEY
MULTITASK WHILE ON A CALL	PRESS THE BLACKBERRY BUTTON WHEN ON A CALL, THEN SELECT THE HOMESCREEN. FROM HERE, YOU CAN ACCESS ANY OTHER APPLICATION AND EMAILS

BLACKBERRY APPLICATIONS

These shortcuts can be used while in apps including Documents to Go and the BlackBerry browser

DESIRED ACTION	SHORTCUT
CHANGE THE SIZE OF A COLUMN IN A SPREADSHEET	PRESS THE W KEY
VIEW THE CONTENTS OF A SPREADSHEET CELL	PRESS SPACE KEY WITH THE CELL HIGHLIGHTED
SEARCH FOR TEXT IN A SPREADSHEET	TAP F FOLLOWED BY THE TEXT YOU'RE LOOKING FOR
SWITCH TO ANOTHER WORKSHEET	PRESS V AND SELECT ANOTHER WORKSHEET
SKIP FORWARDS THROUGH SLIDES	PRESS N
SKIP BACKWARDS THROUGH SLIDES	PRESS P
START A SLIDESHOW	PRESS S
STOP A SLIDESHOW	PRESS ESCAPE
ENTER NEW WEB ADDRESS IN BROWSER	PRESS G
ADD ITEM TO BOOKMARKS	PRESS A
SHOW BOOKMARKS	PRESS K
REFRESH WEB PAGE	PRESS R
SHOW LIST OF LAST WEBSITES VISITED	PRESS I
INSERT BACKSLASH TO A WEB ADDRESS	PRESS SHIFT KEY FOLLOWED BY THE SPACE BUTTON

Tips and tricks

Battery management

Just like other portable electronic devices, the battery life of a PlayBook can vary greatly depending on how it's stored and how it's used. RIM claims its first-generation tablet has a 10-hour battery life, which is pretty impressive.

However, there are a number of things you can do with your BlackBerry smartphone and PlayBook to boost your device's battery life and maximise the amount of time needed between charges.

The table below offers a quick rundown of the average battery life for a range of BlackBerry devices. Modern BlackBerry devices use Li-ion (Lithium-ion) batteries. These are rechargeable and rely on the movement of a lithium ion between the cathode and anode to provide power while in use and while charging.

LAP IT UP
The PlayBook's battery can quickly get drained when you're playing games, but you keep it running for longer by following our tips

DEVICE	AVERAGE TALK TIME (UP TO)	AVERAGE STANDBY TIME (UP TO)
BlackBerry Bold 9700	6 hours	17 days
BlackBerry Bold 9000	4.5 hours	13.5 days
BlackBerry Storm 2	6 hours	11.5 days
BlackBerry Storm 9500	5.5 hours	15 days
BlackBerry Curve 8300, 8310, 8320, 8900	4 hours	17 days
BlackBerry Curve 8520	4.5 hours	17 days
BlackBerry 8800 series	5 hours	22 days
BlackBerry 8700 series 8700g, 8700f, 8700v, 8707g, 8707v	4-5 hours	16 days
BlackBerry PlayBook	10 hours	12.5 days

One of the reasons Li-ion batteries are so popular is because they offer a good weight-to-energy ratio. In addition, they don't adversely affect a device's memory or suffer from energy seepage when they are not being used.

Here are our top six tips for ensuring the engine that powers your device lasts the distance:

1 Ensure the battery is fully charged before first use.

2 Don't wait until the battery is completely dead before recharging. Leaving it to the last minute may mean you don't have your BlackBerry or PlayBook in action when you need it most.

3 Turn off the Wi-Fi and Bluetooth/radio-searching capabilities of your PlayBook if you don't need them. Otherwise, your device will constantly search for connectivity, which wears down the battery.

4 Keep an eye on the backlight brightness on your PlayBook. Reducing it a little won't dramatically affect the display, but it could make a noticeable difference to how long your battery lasts. Use the screen-management controls to adjust the backlight/auto dim/standby timer.

5 Store your BlackBerry smartphone and PlayBook at room temperature. Heated environments make batteries weaker.

6 Social-networking, email and gaming addicts beware! Intensive application use will drain your battery's juice levels quicker than anything else. With the wealth of apps available for BlackBerry smartphones and the PlayBook, resisting the urge to use them all the time will be hard.

Average battery life*

Apple iPad 2

16h 49m

Samsung Galaxy Tab

4h 02m

Motorola Xoom

12h 49m

BlackBerry PlayBook

7h 13m

*Tests conducted by *PC Pro* magazine

Tips and tricks

Documents To Go

You'll find three built-in Microsoft Office-focused applications in the Applications folder of most recent BlackBerry smartphones. These handy apps will also become your PlayBook's best friend.

Word To Go, Sheet To Go and Slideshow To Go form part of the standard Documents To Go suite from DataViz, which lets you view and edit Microsoft Office files on your handset or tablet.

While it's not exactly the same as the full Office experience on a desktop, there's a lot you can do with Documents To Go, and the premium version lets you do even more. Here are some of its main features.

WORD TO GO
- View, edit and new document modes.
- Password-protected file access.
- Integration with the BlackBerry email application for opening attachments.
- Text-editing features, including cut, copy and paste, spellchecking and, in the premium version, advanced character formatting.
- View and edit font types, sizes, colour and styling.
- View tracked changes, with premium users able to add comments.
- Word count.
- The ability to add and delete tables and, in the premium version, add and edit hyperlinks.
- Support for JPG, PNG, BMP, DIB, WMF and EMF graphics formats.
- Support for Documents To Go IT Policy Group in BES 4.1.5.

SLIDESHOW TO GO
- View and edit modes. Premium users can create new files too.
- Slide, Outline and Notes views.
- Read-only file support, with password-protected file access in the premium version.
- Integration with the BlackBerry email application for opening attachments.
- Premium users can view speaker notes and add, duplicate and delete slides.
- JPG, PNG, BMP, DIB, WMF and EMF graphics support.
- Navigation: next/previous slide, go to slide, line/page scrolling in outline view and find function.

SHEET TO GO
- View, edit and new document modes.
- Integration with the BlackBerry email application for opening attachments.
- Password-protected file access.
- Premium users can sort, insert and edit comments and format cells and numbers.
- Navigation functions include find/find next, go to cell, go home and go to end.

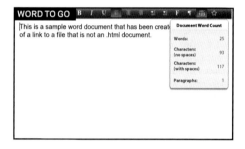

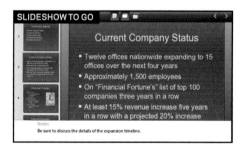

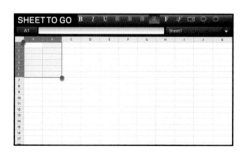

PDF support

Adobe's Portable Document Format (PDF) is an industry-standard technology that encapsulates the text, fonts, graphics and other elements of a document so it can be viewed on any computer, regardless of its hardware, software or operating system.

The PlayBook, like BlackBerry smartphones, supports PDFs, so you can view documents on the device's 1,024x600-pixel screen exactly as they were intended to be viewed. It comes pre-loaded with Adobe's Reader X software, which allows you to view PDF files.

Adobe Reader's interface is slick and intuitive, and it makes perfect use of the PlayBook's gesturing and navigation capabilities. The app includes useful tools such as a highlighter and sticky notes, which make collaborating with others on one document a doddle.

The impressive search function helps you find exactly what you're looking for, whether it's an entire PDF document or a word or a phrase in a document. And less time spent fiddling about looking for what you want means more time creating and editing.

Adobe Reader on the PlayBook is also ideal for consuming rich media on the move, as James Billington, editor of interactive electronic magazine *iGIZMO* explains.

"*iGIZMO* on the BlackBerry PlayBook is interactive, entertaining and more impressive with every read," he said. "Our readers can now engage with ground-breaking photography, video reviews and interactive content on the go – wherever they are and whenever they want to enjoy it."

Business users in particular will benefit from Adobe Reader's advanced functions. Protected mode, for example, enables you to edit and tweak PDF documents in a secure manner without risk of intrusion from malicious code. Other features include:

- High-quality PDF rendering.
- Easy page navigation.
- Quick and easy zooming in and out using pinching and double-tap gestures.
- The ability to change document view from portrait to landscape and vice versa.
- Support for CAD designs and geospatial maps.

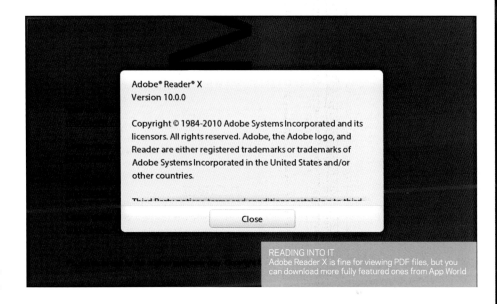

READING INTO IT
Adobe Reader X is fine for viewing PDF files, but you can download more fully featured ones from App World

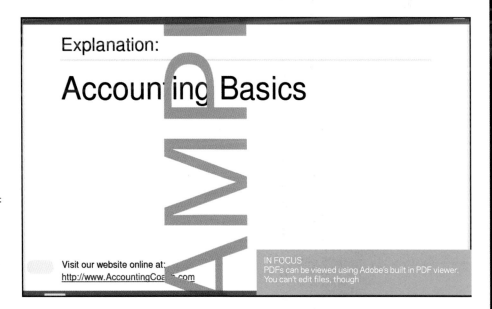

IN FOCUS
PDFs can be viewed using Adobe's built in PDF viewer. You can't edit files, though

The PlayBook isn't just about work – its two cameras mean you'll never miss a photo opportunity again, and it excels at showing off photos and videos and playing music

BLACKBERRY
PLAYBOOK

MULTIMEDIA

CHAPTER
NINE

Camera controls

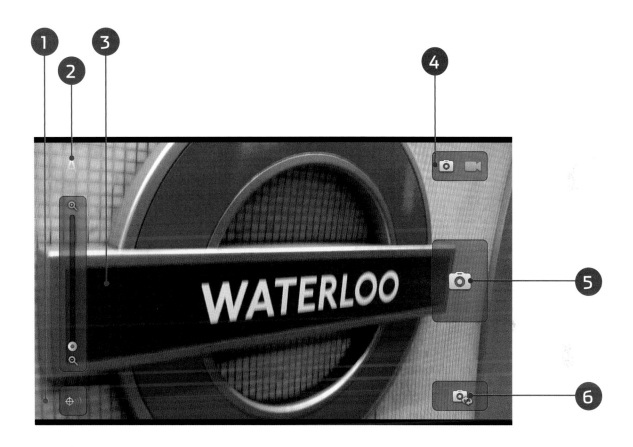

 1 **LOCATION**
You can add location information to each photo you take by tapping this icon. Tap it again to remove the information

 2 **IMAGE MODE**
You can change the image mode from Auto (pictured here) by pulling down the top toolbar and tapping on another mode icon

3 **ZOOM**
Use this bar to zoom in and out of your subject. Just drag your finger up and down the bar until you get the setting you want

 4 **VIDEO/PHOTO**
Switch from the PlayBook's stills camera mode to the video mode and vice versa by tapping this icon

 5 **SHUTTER**
Tap the shutter button once and the photo will be focused and shot. It will be saved automatically to your PlayBook

 6 **SWITCH CAMERAS**
Tap this button to switch between the 3-megapixel front-facing camera and the 5-megapixel rear-facing camera

BLACKBERRY
PLAYBOOK

CHAPTER
NINE

Kobo

BlackBerry

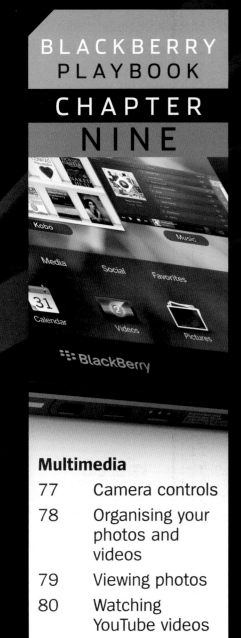

Multimedia

Organising your photos and videos

The BlackBerry PlayBook's 5-megapixel camera is capable of producing stunning shots, and its super-crisp 7-inch screen ensures that every detail in your photos and videos is displayed in vibrant clarity. Here we look at how to organise your snaps and videos so you can show them off in their full glory.

VIEWING YOUR PHOTOS
The PlayBook's Gallery function makes organising and viewing your photos simple.
1. Select the Media tab from the homescreen and choose Photos
2. Your photos are organised into folders. Open the relevant folder and select the image you want to view. The photo will open in a full-screen view
3. Slide your finger to the left or the right to navigate through your photos
4. You can zoom in and out of your shots using multitouch: just pinch your fingers together to zoom out and spread your fingers apart to zoom in
5. Pull down the top bar to see more shots in the folder

VIEWING YOUR VIDEOS
All your videos – whether they're clips you've downloaded or movies you've recorded yourself with the PlayBook's 5-megapixel rear-facing camera – are stored in the Video Gallery. Organising and viewing them is just as straightforward as viewing photos.
1. Select the Media tab from the homescreen and choose Videos
2. The video interface will start up, with tabs along the top. Your videos will appear as thumbnails in a grid view below the tabs, along with their name and the length of the video
3. When you select a video, the thumbnail will enlarge and the video will start playing
4. If you touch the top of the screen while the video is playing, a miniature view of your videos will appear. You can scroll through these using a serious of swipes
5. A scroll bar at the bottom lets you pause, play and stop the video. You can also skip through it by tapping on the timeline scroll bar.

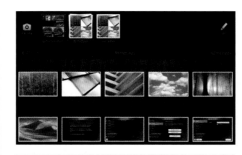

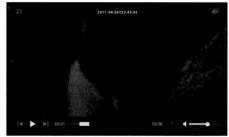

HIDDEN SECRETS
Pulling down from the top of the device reveals a hidden menu that enables you to view all the photos in a folder

Viewing photos

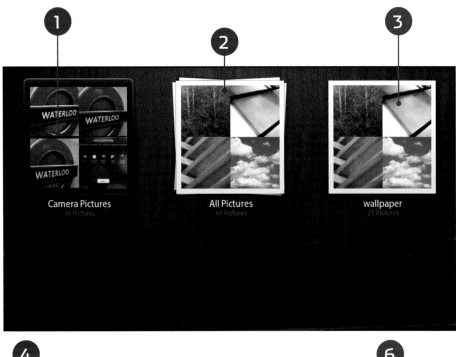

① CAMERA PHOTOS

This displays all the photos you've taken on the PlayBook's camera. Tap on a folder to open the photo full size. You can navigate through them by swiping

② ALL PHOTOS

This displays a slideshow of all your photos, whether you've downloaded them, taken them with the PlayBook's camera or they came preinstalled

③ WALLPAPER

The Wallpaper folder shows all the pictures used as wallpaper. Your PlayBook comes with a selection of preinstalled images that can be used as wallpaper

④ CAMERA

Tapping on the camera icon switches to the PlayBook's camera mode, so you can take a photo

⑤ GALLERY

Pull down the top bar to display this toolbar. Here you can quickly jump between photos

⑥ DELETE

You can delete photos using the rubbish bin icon. This image can't be deleted because it's a preinstalled picture

⑦ SET AS WALLPAPER

This icon allows you to quickly add the selected picture as a wallpaper. It will take a couple of seconds to set

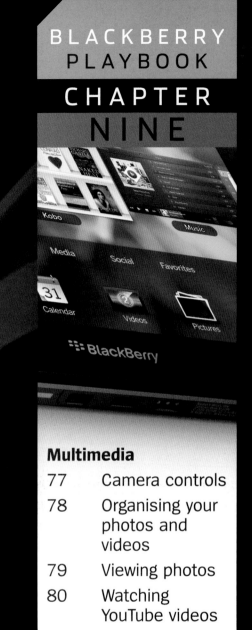

Multimedia

Watching YouTube videos

Although most smartphones and tablets include a YouTube player, the PlayBook's video-streaming functions are all done through the browser, thanks to its superb Flash support.

When you first launch the YouTube website, you'll be presented with the same website you'd see if you were using a computer. You can log into your account if you wish to upload images, or stay logged out if you just want to watch videos.

To search for a specific video, type the name into the search bar. The search results will display in the usual way; just tap the one you want and you'll be taken to a full page where you can start watching.

The video box is rendered to display perfectly on the PlayBook's screen. To start playing the video, just tap on the box.

Just as on the full site, you can tap on the video while it's playing to pause, skip forward or rewind. Everything happens seamlessly, without any pauses, jumps or skips; it's just like watching clips on your computer over a strong Wi-Fi connection.

On the right of the main video window, you'll see a selection of related clips. Tap on any of these to start playing them. You can also log into your YouTube account, view your profile, your channel or other channels you've subscribed to.

YouTube on the PlayBook provides instant access to your favourite videos while on the move. You won't be able to view them when you're away from a data connection, but the PlayBook's screen size makes it perfect for viewing videos when you don't have a computer to hand.

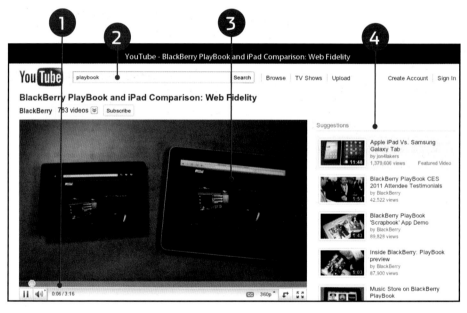

1 VIDEO CONTROLS
Play, pause and scroll through clips using the video controls at the bottom of the screen. It's effortless using your finger to adjust the controls

2 SEARCH
Searching YouTube for videos is as simple on the PlayBook's browser as it is on your computer. Tap on the search bar and the keyboard will pop up

3 MAIN VIDEO
The video will play as close to full size as it can within the Playbook's browser window. You can tap on the main window to pause or play the video

4 RELATED VIDEOS
Just as on the desktop version of YouTube, you can see related videos down the right-hand side of the screen. Just tap on a video to watch it

Listening to music

M usic is an integral part of the multimedia experience. The iPad, with its iPod application, may do it very well, but RIM has made a big effort to integrate music into its tablet, and has managed to do so very successfully.

THE MUSIC LIBRARY

The PlayBook is a great tool for playing and managing your music collection. It supports MP3, AAC, WMA and WAV files, includes a range of tools to make managing your music collection and adding tracks to your library as easy as possible.

To access your music library, select the Media tab on the homescreen and tap Music. Your library is organised by album, and each album will be depicted by thumbnails of the cover. Simply tap on an album and you'll be take to its track listing.

The music player is split into two, with the currently playing track on the left and the track listing on the right. When you start playing a song, the music player controls will appear at the bottom of the screen, allowing you to play, pause and skip to the next track using the scroll bar.

ADDING MUSIC TO YOUR PLAYBOOK

You add music to your PlayBook using the BlackBerry Desktop Software application (see Chapter 4). When you connect your PlayBook to a computer, the software will scan the hard disk for music files wherever they're stored. It doesn't matter whether you use iTunes, Windows Media Player or any other application to organise your library.

Transferring tracks from your computer to your PlayBook couldn't be easier.

1 Plug your PlayBook into your computer using a USB cable. BlackBerry Desktop Software will start automatically.
2 Click on the Media tab in BlackBerry Desktop Software and select Music
3 You can add playlists or synchronise songs by artist or genre. Tick the boxes next to the playlists, artists or genres you want to add to your PlayBook.
4 Alternatively, provided you have enough space on your PlayBook you can synchronise your entire music library by ticking the All music box.
5 To synchronise a random selection of tracks, tick the Random Music box.
6 Once you've selected all the tracks you want to add to your PlayBook, click Sync.

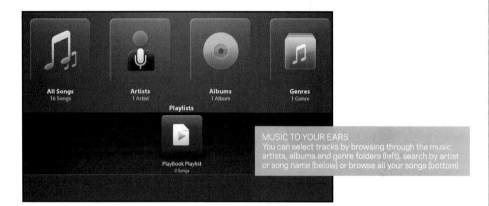

MUSIC TO YOUR EARS
You can select tracks by browsing through the music, artists, albums and genre folders (left), search by artist or song name (below) or browse all your songs (bottom)

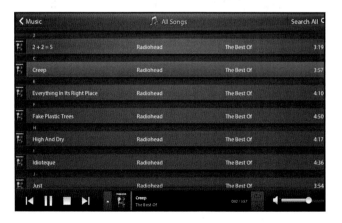

Multimedia

7DIGITAL MUSIC STORE

The 7digital Music Store app is preinstalled on the PlayBook and offers more than 13 million DRM-free MP3s to download. You'll find a link to the store in the Apps section on the homescreen.

When you open the app, you'll see a range of categories such as genres, featured music, new releases and best-sellers. You can also search for a specific artist using the search bar at the top of the screen. You can save a search as a favourite so you can use it again, and you can view all your recent activity from the pull-down menu at the top.

If you're feeling uninspired, you can use 7digital's Recommendation Engine to find music for you. This suggests tracks and artists based on your recent purchasing and browsing history.

Once you've found what you want, click on the album you want to download to bring up the track list. To hear a preview of a track, simply click on it; to buy an album or a track, click on the Buy link. Individual tracks cost 99p, with whole albums available from £3.99. Once you've registered a credit card with the store, you can buy with one-click ordering.

All of 7digital's music is stored on the cloud rather than on your PlayBook, ensuring it's safe. However, you play tracks using the device's music player in the same way as you play songs stored on your PlayBook.

THE PODCAST APP

The Podcast app allows you to browse by content to find a podcast that may interest you. You can subscribe to podcasts if you wish and they'll be updated as new episodes are added. If a podcast has been going for a while, you can also download previous podcasts.

The Podcast app supports both video and audio content. It can also play HD video content, taking advantage of the PlayBook's 1,024x600-pixel screen.

The simple interface makes the app incredibly easy to use. Features and Categories are arranged across the top of the screen, alongside a Downloads tab that shows all your downloaded podcasts. The final tab is My Podcasts, which is your library for organising and playing your files.

A number of third-party podcast apps are available for the PlayBook, but the preinstalled one is free, easy to use and has all the features most people will want, so there seems little point in downloading another.

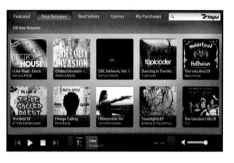

FREE AS A BIRD
The 7digital music store allows you to choose from more than 13 million DRM-free tracks

The Cloud.
Distilled.

Everything you need to know about how
cloud computing will change your business

www.cloudpro.co.uk

From luxury leather cases to portable speakers that fit in the palm of your hand, our selection of accessories will complement your PlayBook perfectly

ACCESSORIES

Cases

The BlackBerry PlayBook is a thing of beauty as well as functionality, so you'll want to protect it from harm with a case that doesn't detract from its shiny good looks or add unnecessary bulk or weight. Here's our pick of those that do the job well, catering for a wide range of tastes and budgets.

NAVITECH HARD GEL CASE

£4.99
FROM WWW.AMAZON.CO.UK

There are plenty of cases available for your PlayBook, but if you've just invested a lot of money in your new device you'll probably want a case that's as kind to your wallet as it is to your tablet.

Enter the hard gel case from Navitech. Your BlackBerry PlayBook fits neatly and snuggly inside the case, so it's still highly portable. The shock and drop protection will keep your PlayBook from harm, while the sleek matt finish and gloss trimming means it looks stylish as well as protected.

Unlike many other budget cases, you'll still be able to use your PlayBook as normal when it's inside the Navitech case. There's a positioned grip to help camera use and cutouts for all ports, so you can charge and dock your device in the usual way when the case is on.

CASE-MATE BARELY THERE HARD CASE COVER

£24.95
FROM WWW.AMAZON.CO.UK

If you're looking for a case for your PlayBook that allows you to access the screen and ports effortlessly, this case cover could be the answer.

It acts just like a stylish second skin, meaning easy access when you want to listen to music on your headphones, take a quick snap with either the front or rear camera or simply charge your tablet.

The Case-Mate Barely There case is made from specially engineered materials, and its impact-resistant, flexible plastic shell covers the back and corners of your BlackBerry Playbook, protecting it from accidental knocks and careless drops.

BLACKBERRY PLAYBOOK SKIN CASE

$19.95 (AROUND £12)
FROM HTTP://CRACKBERRY.COM

Another case that fits your BlackBerry PlayBook like a glove, you'll only know the Skin Case is there because your device will be kept in pristine condition, rather than because it's bulky or unsightly.

The case protects the full exterior of the PlayBook – so you won't need to worry about your shiny new device getting scratched or marked – but still provides easy access to luxurious 7in screen. There are also cutouts around the perimeter of the case for accessing your tablet's ports and buttons.

With a rubber finish, the case feels soft yet solid to the touch, and a non-slip grip means your PlayBook is less likely to slip through clumsy fingers.

Cases

OTTERBOX BLACKBERRY PLAYBOOK DEFENDER

£49.99

FROM WWW.AMAZON.CO.UK

This is one of the more expensive cases available for the PlayBook, but it still offers good value for money.

It's a heavy-duty, three-layered case, designed to protect your device from harm and to keep it looking shiny and free from dust.

Normally when something is dubbed robust it means it looks like a cross between an armadillo and a tank. That's not the case with the OtterBox Defender. It's incredibly sleek and stylish thanks to a polycarbonate shell, silicone skin and transparent protective membrane for the screen. It's also incredibly simple to attach and remove, thanks to the clip-on multidirectional shield and built-in stand.

Silicone plugs ensure you can still access the synchronisation and charging ports with the minimum of fuss, and the rest of the buttons and functions are also easily accessible when the case is on.

BLACKBERRY PLAYBOOK ZIP SLEEVE

£24.99

FROM WWW.AMAZON.CO.UK

If you're using your PlayBook more for work than play and therefore need a stylish, professional-looking case, this Zip Sleeve could be the answer.

Available in black or blue, it looks similar to a personal organiser, meaning it won't look out of place on the boardroom table or in an important contract meeting. And with a smooth fabric outer shell and built-in memory foam innards for added protection, it has substance as well as style.

The design is sleek and slim-fitting, and the zipper ensures easy access to your PlayBook whenever you need it. If you want even more protection, the Zip Sleeve is compatible with other cases too, which is good news for those of us who are particularly accident-prone.

AQUAPAC WATERPROOF CASE FOR BLACKBERRY PLAYBOOK

$42.95 (AROUND £26)

FROM HTTP://CRACKBERRY.COM

We wouldn't recommend going diving with your PlayBook, but if you often find yourself working outside – or simply taking photos of the kids on the beach – you'll need a waterproof case to protect your tablet from the elements.

Waterproof to a depth of 15ft, the Aquapac Waterproof Case for BlackBerry PlayBook is resistant to salt water and UV sunlight. It's also dust- and sand-proof, so it's ideal for those holiday snaps by the sea.

The case comprises a durable, waterproof plastic sheath and a patented Aquaclip Locking Closure System, and you can use your PlayBook while it's in the case through a special window. It also comes with a carry strap.

PDAIR BLACKBERRY PLAYBOOK LEATHER FLIP CASE

$58 (AROUND £35)

FROM WWW.PDAIR.COM

Seasoned BlackBerry smartphone users will probably be familiar with this flip-style holder. The PDair BlackBerry PlayBook Leather Flip Case takes the styling favoured by many manufacturers for smartphone cases and essentially scales it up to accommodate the PlayBook.

Made out of leather and finished with high-quality white stitching, the PDair BlackBerry PlayBook Leather Flip Case has a luxurious look and feel and is ideal for busy professionals who need to take their PlayBook with them on the move but also need to ensure it doesn't get damaged.

Handy cut-outs ensure that your PlayBook's key ports and functions can be accessed quickly and easily while it's in the case, and a handy belt clip means you can effortlessly carry your device around with you.

BELKIN 12" CLASSIC SLEEVE

£19.35

FROM WWW.MOBILEFUN.CO.UK

The BlackBerry PlayBook is no cheap toy. It may offer a whole host of features and functions for the price, but it's still a hefty enough expense to warrant a casing that will keep it safe and sound.

The Belkin 12" Classic Sleeve offers just that kind of peace of mind. With a Koskin leather-effect exterior, it exudes an air of understated elegance as well, while the soft microfibre lining means you won't need to worry about your device being scratched.

The fastening mechanism prevents your PlayBook falling out while you're on the move, and accessing your PlayBook is easy whenever you need it. With a price under £20, this sleek black casing is a great buy.

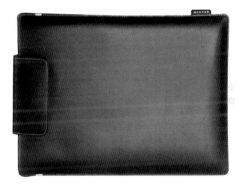

PIEL FRAMA iMAGNUM FOR BLACKBERRY PLAYBOOK

£61.95

FROM WWW.MOBILEFUN.CO.UK

It may be expensive, but this stunning hand-made case from the Piel Frama iMagnum range will complement the beauty of your PlayBook perfectly.

Available in either black or tan and made from high-quality leather with a soft leather lining and polypropylene inner layer, this case will envelope your PlayBook with tender loving care and protection. The strong Gutermann thread adds even more strength to its already elegant look.

Given the high level of precision and workmanship that goes into each case, you'll have to wait 25 days for one to be produced by Piel Frama's dedicated team of leather artisans. But it'll certainly be worth the wait.

Stands

Although the BlackBerry PlayBook is a highly portable device, designed for use on the move, sometimes you may want to stay in one place to use it. A dedicated stand will provide stability and make extended use more comfortable. Here's our pick of the best support acts for your PlayBook.

SPIDER PODIUM UNIVERSAL TABLET DESK STAND
£24.95
FROM WWW.MOBILEFUN.CO.UK

Stands don't have to be boring, as this podium stand from Spider proves. As the name suggests, it looks like a spider but, unlike the creepy crawlies, once your PlayBook is attached to one of these stands it isn't going anywhere.

Lightweight, compact and ultra-portable, the Spider Podium Universal Tablet Desk Stand is functional as well as funky. It can be moulded into any position to stand on any surface, so as well as being used on your desk you can attach it to your car or even a bike. Cutouts are provided so your device can be charged while it's on the stand, so you won't have any trouble refuelling your PlayBook.

It's designed to work with a wide range of portable devices, including the Amazon Kindle and the iPad 2, so if you have other tablets this is the stand for you.

AMZER FOLDO STAND UP
$16.95 (AROUND £10)
FROM WWW.AMAZON.COM

This stand looks a bit like an artist's easel, and put the PlayBook on it and you'll be able to create your own masterpieces, whether they be work documents, photos, videos or artwork.

The appeal of the Amzer Foldo stand lies in its portability. It's a travel-friendly stand that weighs just 82g, meaning you can take it anywhere.

Non-skid cushioned pads on the legs also provide plenty of stability, making it ideal for using on the train or simply freeing up your hands for lunch! It also enables you to use your PlayBook while it's in a case.

BLACKBERRY PLAYBOOK RAPID CHARGING STAND
£59.99
FROM WWW.AMAZON.CO.UK

The idea of buying a portable device is so that you can access it quickly and easily while you're on the move. However, often you'll want to use your PlayBook when you're nowhere near a power socket, so ensuring your device is always powered up and ready to go is key.

This rapid charging stand from RIM powers up your PlayBook twice as fast as traditional chargers. Simply slip your BlackBerry PlayBook into the dock, plug it in and you're away. You can continue using your device while it's charging thanks to the stand's design, which places it at the optimal angle for watching videos or reading documents.

Chargers

O n the opposite page we highlighted the BlackBerry PlayBook Rapid Charging Stand, which allows you to use your tablet while it's charging, but a number of other power options are also available. We've also looked at a device that boosts your PlayBook's signal so you can use it wherever you may be.

BLACKBERRY PLAYBOOK RAPID TRAVEL CHARGER

£59.99
FROM WWW.AMAZON.CO.UK

Another travel-friendly companion, this charger is extremely compact, and has been designed to complement the panache of the PlayBook itself.

The two-metre long cable means you'll be able to place your PlayBook a reasonable distance away from the power socket and still use it while it's charging. Not that you'll need to leave your PlayBook plugged in for long: with a power output of 24W, the Rapid Travel Charger will power up your device twice as fast as a standard charger. It automatically reacts to your PlayBook's battery levels, so it will receive optimum charging.

It's not the cheapest charger available, but it's stylish and provides one of the fastest and easiest ways to boost your PlayBook's power when you're out and about.

COMPACT USB CAR CHARGER ADAPTER FOR BLACKBERRY PLAYBOOK

£18.49
FROM WWW.FOMMY.CO.UK

You can charge your mobile phone while you're in your car, so why not do the same with your BlackBerry PlayBook? This compact USB car charger adapter allows you to do just that.

At just 54x24mm, it's extremely portable, and it's also incredibly easy to use: simply plug it into your car's power socket/cigarette lighter and connect it to the PlayBook's USB port. Compatible with most standard in-car power sockets and cigarette lighters, it can also charge your mobile phone, MP3 player, GPS unit or any other gadget capable of being charged via USB.

CELL PHONE SIGNAL BOOSTER STICKER

$4.99 (AROUND £3)
FROM WWW.ACCESSORYGEEKS.COM

It's a familiar problem: you're out and about and really need to make a call on your mobile or use the internet, only to find the signal is too weak. You curse the air, blame the networks and generally feel frustrated.

This handy little sticker puts an end to those frustrations by using a magnetic field to boost your mobile device's signal. Simply stick it on the battery or your PlayBook's chassis and watch the signal bars shoot up!

Compatible with most mobile phones, this incredibly cheap solution also reduces static, thus boosting call clarity. However, it doesn't perform miracles: it can't boost a signal where there isn't one to start with.

Other accessories

So enamoured with your PlayBook that you can't bear to be parted with it when you're in the car? Want to blast out music around the house, use your tablet while lounging in the sun or protect its screen from scratches and marks? These in-car accessories, screen protectors and speakers could be just the ticket.

IGRIP BLACKBERRY PLAYBOOK WINDSHIELD MOUNT
PRICE TBC
FROM WWW.MOBILEFUN.CO.UK

If you drive regularly and need directions or you'd like your favourite tunes piped through the car while you're travelling – or if you're a passenger and simply want to be entertained – this windshield mount could prove very helpful indeed.

The iGrip BlackBerry PlayBook Windshield Mount is a great way of keeping your tablet close to you on the move. Once attached to your dashboard, you can adjust the device to view it in either landscape or portrait mode, and rotate it 360 degrees to get the viewing position just right.

A dual support suction mount provides stability while driving and minimises the impact of road vibrations, while your PlayBook is kept safely in the holder by four mounting points and a safety switch to lock them in place.

IGRIP BLACKBERRY PLAYBOOK HEADREST MOUNT
PRICE TBC
FROM WWW.MOBILEFUN.CO.UK

This headrest mount has been certified by BlackBerry under its Built for BlackBerry scheme. It attaches securely to most car seats and is a great way to keep little ones – or big kids – entertained in the back of the car.

A quick release mechanism allows your PlayBook to be attached and removed in seconds, and once in place, the swivel action ensures users can benefit from optimum viewing angles.

The holder can also be used as a standalone case for your PlayBook, and it comes with an adjustable integrated stand so you can use on your desk, too.

TRU PROTECTION ANTI-GLARE SCREEN FILM FOR BLACKBERRY PLAYBOOK
£19.95
FROM WWW.MOBILEFUN.CO.UK

Many screen protectors end up making the display look smudged, but Tru Protection's Anti-Glare Screen Film uses cutting-edge technology and quality materials to protect your PlayBook's screen and enhance your viewing experience.

Advanced static cling adhesive makes it easy to apply, and an anti-glare finish ensures fingerprints and reflections are minimised, so you'll be able to use your PlayBook in almost any lighting conditions.

The film is just as easy to remove and doesn't leave any nasty residue, so you don't need to worry if you accidentally put it in the wrong place first time around and need to apply it again. Two screen films are included in the pack.

INVISIBLESHIELD SCREEN PROTECTOR FOR BLACKBERRY PLAYBOOK

£25.48

FROM WWW.MOBILEDEN.CO.UK

Even if you're the most careful of users marks and scratches can spoil your pristine display, but the InvisibleSHIELD Screen Protector for BlackBerry PlayBook can keep your tablet looking as good as new no matter how badly you treat it.

Custom-built for the BlackBerry PlayBook, the InvisibleSHIELD certainly lives up to its name: you'll only know it's there because you applied it and because of the lack of marks and scratches.

Durability is at the heart of the InvisibleSHIELD's design. Made from clear urethane – which originated in the US military, where it was employed to protect the edges of helicopter blades – this is one of the toughest protectors on the market, yet it's easy to apply and remove.

SOUNDM8 MICRO PORTABLE SPEAKERS

£12.95

FROM WWW.MOBILEFUN.CO.UK

The PlayBook may be primarily a business device, but its multimedia capabilities mean it's ideal for entertainment as well. However, if you want to listen to music and watch movies you'll need more oomph than the built-in speakers can provide – and you won't want to be lugging a huge set of speakers around with you.

The tiny SoundM8 Micro Portable Speakers are just 50x50x35mm in size so will easily slip into your pocket, yet their 360-degree sound field and a vacuum bass middle means they sound better than speakers five times their size, while a rechargeable Li-ion battery provides up to eight hours of music playback.

BASS BUDDY POP-OPEN SPEAKERS SYSTEM

£8.90

FROM WWW.AMAZON.CO.UK

This low-cost speaker system may look a little like a yo-yo, but it delivers much more fun than a wheel on a thread.

Small and compact, this highly portable set has been designed with mobile users in mind, and will make listening to music on your PlayBook a real pleasure.

The Bass Buddy Pop-Open Speakers System uses Tru-bass technology to deliver deep, rich bass tones through the unique pop-open mechanism. It comes with a built-in rechargeable battery and a USB charging cable, while a 3.5mm jack ensures compatibility with a range of MP3 players and smartphones, not just your BlackBerry PlayBook.

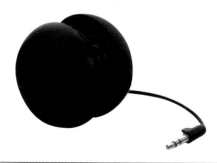

We predict what the future holds for the PlayBook - and reveal what we'd like to see in the next version of the BlackBerry tablet

BLACKBERRY PLAYBOOK

CHAPTER ELEVEN

THE FUTURE

A tablet-shaped future

Portable computing platforms are undoubtedly becoming increasingly popular, but there's both good and bad news for when it comes to the future for the industry. Let's get the bad news out of the way first. Things aren't looking good for netbooks, if analyst and market predictions are anything to go by.

The PC market is expected to grow by 14 per cent in 2011, with much of that boost accredited to tablet devices, according to research firm Canalys. The change will span both the consumer and business worlds and, according to the research firm, it will be most pronounced in developed markets such as the UK, US, France, Germany and Japan.

Canalys analyst Tim Coulling said that tablets' innovative user experience had "captured the imagination of consumers, who are extending the life of their existing hardware, while taking an interest in tablets".

Fellow analyst Gartner predicts tablets will continue to eat into the netbooks market. In March 2011, the company lowered its forecast for PC unit shipments for 2011 to an increase of 10.5 per cent over 2010 (down from its original prediction of a 15.9 per cent increase) and to a rise of 13.6 per cent in 2012 (down from its original prediction of 14.8 per cent), citing a predicted weakening in demand.

"These results reflect marked reductions in expected near-term unit growth based on expectations of weaker consumer mobile PC demand, in no small

part because of the near-term weakness expected in China's mobile PC market, but also because of a general loss in consumer enthusiasm for mobile PCs," said Ranjit Atwal, Gartner's research director.

The place previously occupied in consumers' hearts by PCs will be filled by other devices such as tablets, according to fellow Gartner research director George Shiffler.

"We expect growing consumer enthusiasm for mobile PC alternatives, such as the iPad and other media tablets, to dramatically slow home mobile PC sales, especially in mature markets," he said.

"We once thought that mobile PC growth would continue to be sustained by consumers buying second and third mobile PCs as personal devices. However, we now believe that consumers are not only likely to forgo additional mobile PC buys but are also likely to extend the lifetimes of the mobile PCs they retain as they adopt media tablets and other mobile PC alternatives as their primary mobile device.

"Overall, we now expect home mobile PCs to average less than 10 per cent annual growth in mature markets from 2011 through 2015."

But what about the business world? Gartner believes the professional PC market will enjoy double-digit growth in 2011 and 2012, but it won't be immune to the lure of the tablet either.

"Even in the professional market, media tablets are being considered as PC substitutes, likely at least delaying some PC replacements," said Raphael Vasquez, senior research analyst at Gartner.

RIM has traditionally been very strong in the corporate arena, and aims to build on that solid foundation with the first-generation PlayBook. Uncertainty remains over the extent to which business users will take to tablet devices, however.

Canalys believes a clear opportunity exists for tablet manufacturers in the corporate arena. "The number of affluent, highly mobile executives buying tablets will increase quickly in 2011," said principal analyst Daryl Chiam.

"Likewise, vertical market adoption of tablets, especially in healthcare and education, will gain momentum, as more appropriate applications are built," said Chiam.

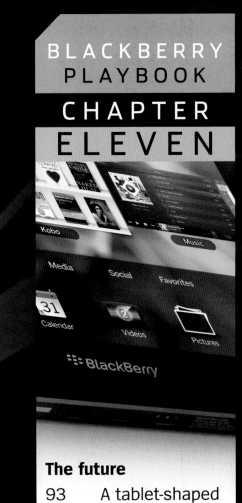

BlackBerry

The future

PlayBook 2: a wishlist

Technology consumers are a demanding group, and invariably expect every single bell and whistle they've ever dreamed of as soon as a product is announced. The BlackBerry PlayBook is an innovative product and a highly capable device, but it's RIM's first foray into tablet territory. The first-generation iPad lacked features many users thought it should have had from the outset, and we had to wait for the iPad 2 to see some of those improvements. RIM deserves the same courtesy.

One example of what we'd like to see in the future is support for native apps. Currently you can only use the email, calendaring and BlackBerry Messenger applications via a Bridge connection with your BlackBerry smartphone. We'd like to see support for those apps on the PlayBook for those that don't have a BlackBerry or don't have their phone to hand for whatever reason.

Ensuring these apps are usable without the need for a BlackBerry smartphone would go some way to answering those doubters who have questioned how successful the PlayBook can be in its current form.

Brian Blair, principal and equity analyst at Wedge Partners, suggested the PlayBook could end up costing RIM millions of dollars. In an interview published by CNBC, Blair said the PlayBook would be "inferior to other tablets on the market and consumers won't buy it". Asked to describe the product in one word, he replied, "Misguided".

We'd also like to see RIM building on the solid foundation it's already created in terms of app speed. The PlayBook has a speedy 1GHz dual-core processor, but in the future we'd expect RIM to take things to the next level. Texas Instruments' OMAP4440 dual-core processor, for instance, provides speeds of up to 1.5GHz per CPU core.

There's also the question of memory. Currently the PlayBook comes with 1GB of RAM. This is more than enough for most users' needs, but RIM will need to keep pace with user demand and its rivals' offerings.

Finally, the front-facing 3-megapixel camera and rear-facing five-megapixel camera are fine for a first-generation device, but we'd expect higher megapixel counts in the next iteration.

The BlackBerry PlayBook's software is also a first for RIM. A tablet operating system essentially designed from the ground up will no doubt get better with age. That's not to say the first generation isn't impressive, but updates and newer versions are sure to bring new and improved features. Future support for Android apps is also welcome and will add to the PlayBook's appeal both to users and developers.

Lastly, it would be good to see other flavours of the PlayBook emerge, much as the BlackBerry smartphone lineup includes different devices for different types of users at a range of price points. A choice of PlayBooks would undoubtedly help broaden the potential market for the device.

Next steps

On the opposite page we've focused on what we'd like to see in future versions of the PlayBook, but what do we know for certain about the device's future?

Apps have been a major factor in the success of the iPhone and iPad, and RIM is hoping Android apps will provide similar mass appeal for its device. As well as apps created specifically for the PlayBook, it will feature an app player capable of running software created for Android 2.3 and above.

Mike Lazaridis, RIM's president and co-chief executive, claims the PlayBook will provide "one of the most compelling app experiences available in a mobile computing device today... The addition of BlackBerry Java and Android apps for the PlayBook on BlackBerry App World will provide our users with an even greater choice of apps and showcase the versatility of the platform," he said.

The company is also focusing on development, with support for Adobe Flash, AIR, C/C++ HTML5 and Java. Jim Tobin, senior vice-president of the software, services and enterprise markets business unit, said RIM was planning "a range of advanced cloud-based services, advanced location-based services, application analytics and powerful Push services".

With Apple's second-generation iPad and Motorola's Xoom device already available and a slew of rivals launching products over the coming months, the BlackBerry PlayBook faces stiff competition. For RIM to keep pace in the tablet race, it will need to continue innovating.

TIME TRAVELLER
What can BlackBerry bring out next to compete against the other leading tablet manufacturers?

Glossary

Bandwidth
The data capacity of a connection. A higher bandwidth can transmit more data over a given period of time.

BES
BlackBerry Enterprise Server. A software plug-in for the most popular business email servers (Microsoft Exchange, Lotus Domino) that synchronises email, calendar and address-book information between the server and any BlackBerry devices authorised to communicate with it.

BIS
BlackBerry Internet Service. Allows BlackBerry users to access the internet and POP3/IMAP email accounts without connecting through a BES. The service is usually provided by mobile phone operators.

Bluetooth
A wireless standard that enables data connections between electronic devices such as desktop computers, mobile phones, hands-free headsets and remote controls, usually within a 10m range, although some devices support over 100m.

Bridging
The term applied to connecting your BlackBerry smartphone with your PlayBook. It allows you to use the server services on your PlayBook, such as email, calendars and BlackBerry Messenger. The PlayBook is unable to access any of these features without bridging.

Capacitive
A capacitive screen is designed to be controlled by a finger rather than a stylus and differs from a resistive touchscreen in that it requires electric signals from your finger to work. Capacitive screens are generally more responsive than resistive screens and can't be used with a regular stylus.

EDGE
Enhanced Data for GSM Evolution. This system can provide near-3G data rates on a GSM network. Speeds of up to 384Kbps are possible.

GPRS
General Packet Radio Service. An 'always on' data connection for GSM mobile-phone services.

GPS
Global Positioning System. A receiver that communicates with satellites orbiting the earth to determine the position of people and objects on the ground.

GSM
Global System for Mobile communications. The most widely used digital mobile system and Europe's de facto wireless telephone standard.

HSDPA
High-Speed Downlink Packet Access. An 'always on' improvement on standard 3G/UMTS data services. Offers download rates of up to 14.4Mbps, though most networks in the UK and the US offer 1.8, 3.6 or 7.2Mbps.

IMAP
Internet Message Access Protocol, also known as IMAP4. An improved standard for email used by consumers and businesses. Allows for multiple server-side folders and virtual mailboxes. Mail is retained on the server and synchronised with the client, so you always have access to the same emails. IMAP is the system behind most popular webmail services.

Java
Industry-standard object-oriented programming language and virtual machine, invented by Sun Microsystems. Popular as a platform for mobile apps because it can run as a virtual machine, making applications

hardware-independent and able to run on devices from different manufacturers.

OS
Operating system. The core software, also referred to as firmware, that allows a device to function.

PIM
Personal Information Manager. A software application that functions as a personal organiser.

POP
Post Office Protocol, also known as POP3. The most common and basic form of email account. Messages are downloaded from a server to the client from a single mailbox.

SIM
Subscriber Identity Module. A SIM card is the smartcard in all GSM and 3G mobiles. It identifies the user account to the network and provides data storage for basic user and network information, such as contacts.

UMTS
Universal Mobile Telecommunications System. The European version of the 3G wireless phone system. Offers data rates of up to 384Kbps.

VoIP
Voice over Internet Protocol. The process by which voice telephone calls are made and carried across a data network rather than a conventional telephone system. Popular VoIP services include Skype, Vonage and Google Talk. Long-distance and international calls are usually much cheaper using VoIP than a conventional phone system.

Wi-Fi
Generic term commonly used for wireless LAN technology, also known as 802.11a, b, g and n. Wi-Fi is a trademark of the Wi-Fi Alliance, which ensures the wireless compatibility of hardware.